VICTORIAN STUDIES

GARLAND REFERENCE LIBRARY
OF THE HUMANITIES
(VOL. 1068)

VICTORIAN STUDIES
A Research Guide

Sharon W. Propas

GARLAND PUBLISHING, INC. • NEW YORK & LONDON
1992

Library of Congress Cataloging-in-Publication Data

Propas, Sharon W., 1947–
  Victorian studies : a research guide / Sharon W. Propas.
    p.   cm. — (Garland reference library of the humanities ; vol.
  1068)
  Includes index.
  ISBN 0-8240-5840-2
  1. Great Britain—History—Victoria, 1837–1901—Bibliography.
  2. Great Britain—Civilization—19th century—Bibliography.
  I. Title. II. Series.
  Z2019.P76 1992
  [DA550]
  016.941—dc20   91-45048
                                                      CIP

Printed on acid-free, 250-year-life paper
Manufactured in the United States of America

To the memory of my mother,

Marjorie E. Weiss

CONTENTS

Contents

Preface

This work grew out of a combination of my own studies in Victorian literature and many years of assisting library users in research libraries. I have observed, both in my own research and in helping others, that questions falling firmly into a particular discipline are generally much easier to answer than those crossing disciplinary lines. First, library organization assumes that research will respect disciplinary boundaries. All the monographic and many of the serial works by and about Browning, for example, will be in one place, facilitating browsing and a serendipitous approach to research. In contrast, a researcher wishing to compare the artistic depiction of colonialism with popular attitudes toward the Empire will find the materials widely scattered across four or five call-number divisions. In addition, many research collections in university library systems are divided into smaller departmental collections, necessitating visits to many libraries. Those wishing to find resources for such a cross-disciplinary subject need to have a good idea of what they are looking for before entering the library stacks. Even serendipity takes some planning when materials are widely scattered.

Second, only recently have reference tools directly addressed the problems of finding materials across disciplines. Victorianists have been fortunate in having one of the earliest and best cross-disciplinary guides to research, Lionel Madden's *How to Find Out About the Victorian Period* (see item 69). However, in the twenty years since this invaluable guide appeared, much has changed in Victorian studies and indeed in all fields of academic research. Interdisciplinary fields have multiplied and gained legitimacy, becoming to an increasing extent the foundation for undergraduate education. New fields have influenced and modified more traditional fields of study. And in a combination of events especially important for a guide to research, an unprecedented explosion has taken place in academic publishing, and the computer has become an important tool in controlling this flood of information. Where Madden's task was to find a few sources for many fields, the more common problem now is to distinguish among the many reference tools available and to identify the most complete and dependable. Scholars need to be aware of the tools now available in various print and electronic formats.

This guide attempts to address these needs as they pertain to all aspects of the study of the Victorian period. "Victorian" is here defined as the period from 1832 to 1900 in Great Britain, Ireland, and the countries of the British Empire. Sources on the countries of the Empire are given only when they directly relate to the relationship between Britain and these nations. I have assumed that those using this guide will already have basic library skills and will be familiar with at least one research library.   Since the humanities have been comparatively slow to embrace information technology, and a majority of Victorianists come from a humanities background, I have assumed less familiarity with electronic information resources. My intended audience includes graduate students beginning in-depth research for the first time and more seasoned scholars who need some assistance in identifying sources for disciplines other than their own.

The materials selected for the bibliography include both reference works specifically on the Victorian period and more general reference works in which some part is useful to the Victorianist. By a "reference work," I mean those books, microforms, periodicals, and databases offering information in summary or overview form, such as encyclopedias; short answers, such as dictionaries and almanacs; and guides and lists of research sources, such as research guides and bibliographies. I have attempted to be comprehensive through 1989 for sources on various aspects of the Victorian period. The more general works also date through 1989, with the criteria that the work have information on Victorian studies or applicable to Victorian studies and not easily obtainable elsewhere. All sources are in English. The largest number of the entries are for monographs, titles published separately rather than as a part of a periodical or a series. I have listed several annually published bibliographies, both those appearing in book form and those appearing in an issue of a journal. I have also listed a few one-time bibliographies appearing in periodicals, when they offer especially valuable material. Many reference works appear as parts of series. From these series, I have included individual titles of interest to those in Victorian studies and indicated in the citation the series title. I have also included works in various electronic formats, including microforms, online databases, and CD-ROMs.

Several categories of material have been excluded for either reasons of space or of audience. Plot summaries and elementary guides to the use of the library are generally addressed to undergraduates and have been omitted for that reason. Narrative historical surveys, such as the various

Oxford and Cambridge histories, have also been omitted. Though these types of surveys have important reference uses, there are too many fine overviews of the Victorian period in too many subject fields for their inclusion in a brief guide. Similarly, since all primary texts have been omitted in print form, I have also not covered the subject of full-text databases. The only primary materials included in this bibliography are in microform. The criteria for their inclusion are covered in the introduction to that section. Finally, bibliographies and other reference works devoted to a single person have been excluded for obvious reasons of space. However, many indexes and bibliographies listing single-person bibliographies have been included so that the researcher may track down these valuable sources.

Organization presented some problem, since I wanted to present a truly cross-disciplinary picture of the resources available to the researcher in Victorian studies. However, after experimenting with several arrangements by reference type, such as placing all dictionaries together regardless of their subject, I realized that I was fighting the natural arrangement of this material by discipline and that the result was more confusing than enlightening. I have therefore followed the common arrangement of listing general reference sources first. I have then listed some of the sources covering interdisciplinary studies or more than one discipline. The largest section of the bibliography is divided by discipline. Each of the larger areas is subdivided by type of reference work or by a subdivision of the subject field. Some use a combination of division by type of reference work and by subject. Sections vary in their subsections according to the types of works available and the logic of the subject. Within the subdivisions, titles are arranged by original date of publication, with the oldest title first. Within subject sections having five or fewer entries, I have not included subdivisions but have arranged material in date order. The one section devoted to a single format is that describing microforms sets.

Each entry gives a full bibliographic citation for the items covered. More than one item may be included in an entry when later volumes are updates or supplements of the main title under discussion. Each entry is annotated. At the minimum, I have attempted to give some idea of the organization and usefulness of the source. Some materials, those whose use is obvious and whose information is dependable, receive only a brief description. Other items seem to call for longer comments. Those sources with an important history or those presenting special problems to the user have received longer annotations. Though not all of the annotations are evaluative, items of outstanding importance or quality or those presenting major problems or inaccuracies are noted. Information on databases is included in the entry on the database's print analog. Important databases not having print analogs are covered at the end of the bibliography under Electronic Formats

A wide variety of resources has been used to compile this bibliography. Madden's *How to Find Out About the Victorian Period* has provided the starting point for further research. I have included the titles he covered only when they remain of importance for current research and were available to me for examination. Therefore this bibliography supplements rather than supersedes Madden's work. Titles published after Madden's guide and some that he did not include have been drawn from a variety of sources, all of which have been included in this bibliography.

Acknowledgments

I would like to thank the libraries of the University of Cincinnati and of Stanford University for their support during the writing of this bibliography. Both by employing me and by providing me with excellent collections on which to base my research, they made this book possible. At both libraries, the Interlibrary Loan Departments performed wonders in obtaining the unobtainable, allowing me to examine materials I would not have seen otherwise. I am especially grateful to the Associates of The Stanford University Library for establishing the David C. Weber Grant for the support of research by librarians and to the members of the committee who awarded me this grant.

Part I:

Using the Library

Research Strategy

Research strategy is nothing more than an efficient plan for finding the information you need. Such strategies can differ depending on the subject to be researched and the degree of knowledge you already possess, but in general, a good research strategy has two goals: to work toward specific knowledge from general knowledge and to prevent the researcher from having to repeat steps in a search.

1.   Definition.

The first step in planning your research is to know what topic you are researching and how much you wish to know about it. This step may seem too obvious to even need stating, but its lack is the cause of a good deal of wasted time in research libraries. First, clearly state what you want to know or to prove. Do not at this stage speculate on where the material may be found or on what the information will be. Once you know what it is that you need, give some thought to the level of information you want. Do you need one specific fact or a large body of information?   How much do you already know about your topic? Will you be needing some broad, background information to further narrow your topic or can you start with more advanced and specific materials? Do you know, generally, how much material is available on this topic? Are you exploring a new area or is there a vast amount already written on the topic? These questions will help you in determining how extensive your research need be and at what level of expertise you should begin.

2.   Look at background sources.

Once these questions are answered, you can begin the next step, which will also help to further define your topic. If you have little information on the subject you are pursuing, are in need of a context for the information you already have, or wish to further narrow your topic, you will need to examine some background sources. Encyclopedic works of all kinds can provide most of the information you will need at this point, and, for this reason, are listed at the beginning of the various sections of this bibliography, after guides to research. Many of the more scholarly encyclopedias will also provide a start on the next research step by providing a brief bibliography of seminal works on the subject being discussed.

Some background sources can also provide valuable information about manuscript and archival resources. Check the bibliographies in these sources for mentions of unpublished materials on the documents. If this step does not provide this information, you may need to go to the sources listed in this bibliography on archives and special collections. The bibliographies on your subject are another potential source of information on locating unpublished materials.

3.   Compile a preliminary bibliography of books on the topic.

If you have consulted a scholarly encyclopedia for the previous step or if you have some familiarity with your subject area, you should already have a basic list of some of the most important books on your topic. At this point you will need to consult library catalogs and subject bibliographies for additional books. The section in this guide on catalogs will assist you in understanding the structure of print and online library catalogs and will discuss the way in which subject headings are used by libraries. A large part of this bibliography is devoted to the various bibliographies available on Victorian topics. The section following this discussion of research strategy describes some of the characteristics of bibliographies and will assist you in using them to their greatest advantage.

In using both catalogs and bibliographies, it is of utmost importance that you take down the most complete bibliographic citation available to you and the source in which you found the citation. This will save you time and much backtracking if you need to use interlibrary loan or the catalogs of several libraries. Though you will have to confirm this information from the source itself, it is also useful in compiling your final bibliography. You will be assured that you have all of the necessary information and will not have to try to recreate your research process at the point when you should be almost done.

4.   Compile a preliminary bibliography of articles on your subject.
The extent of the work you have to do for this step will depend on the amount of information you already have. Again, the bibliographies mentioned in the last step can be of great assistance. Some bibliographies, however, do not include periodical articles, and, in any case, you will want to update the material listed beyond the bibliography's cut-off date. The various indexes and abstracts that will be necessary for this step are listed in the main body of this guide. Be sure to take down a full citation and the source of this citation. For the purposes of interlibrary loan or any other search for the locations of material, this full information is even more important than in a search for a book.

5.   Locate and evaluate the sources.

At this stage, you begin to accumulate the sources with which you will be working. First obtain the materials immediately available to you in local libraries. As you obtain each source, you should make the first cut in eliminating irrelevant works. Examine tables of contents and indexes for the presence of material you can use. Scan the sections which seem to address your topic and gain a sense of where and how this material will fit into your knowledge and interpretation of your subject. If the material seems useful, examine the bibliographic citations in the book or article for further sources.

The process of obtaining materials not locally available to you should also be started at this point. Major repositories of materials should be identified and interlibrary loan requests should be initiated.   Means for gaining access to materials not obtainable through interlibrary loan should be explored. If you need to visit an archive or other special collection, this is a good point to write letters of inquiry, so you will know early in the research process which of the materials needed for your project will be available to you. If you are unable to travel to these materials, ascertain whether copying services are available and their cost.

6.   Locate and evaluate new materials.

This step is essentially a duplicate of step 5. Track down and evaluate any new materials located through the citations found in the books and articles in your preliminary bibliography. Continue the process of using the citations in the material you have located until you are satisfied with the completeness of your research.

7. Begin to read and take notes from material.

This step is both the first step of the writing process and the final step of the research process. At this time you should be sure to confirm from the title pages of your sources the citations you have taken down from your bibliographic sources. The process of reading and note-taking should also enable you to make a final evaluation of the completeness of your research. This is the point at which you can most effectively fill in any gaps in information or opinion. Again, a number of questions may help you know whether your research is now complete. Have I seen material on all sides of a question or debate? Have I looked at the most commonly cited sources on this subject? Have I answered all of the questions I had at the beginning of my research? Can I say I have a good idea of the state of scholarly opinion on this subject? If you can answer "yes" to all of these questions, you have completed your research and are ready to begin organizing your material for writing.

Library Catalogs

Library catalogs come in many forms. Book catalogs, card catalogs, microfiche catalogs, CD-ROM catalogs, and online catalogs can all be found in the course of a lengthy research project if you visit many libraries. The older the catalog, the less likely it will conform to any of the national or international standards followed by most libraries today and the more likely it is to be based on its own set of filing rules and subject headings. However, these idiosyncratic catalogs are rapidly being replaced. You will find that most research libraries have a card catalog, an online catalog, or some combination of the two. I will therefore confine my discussion to the ways in which these two types of catalog are organized and to features which they have in common.

Subject Searching. All but the most specialized library catalogs allow some access by subject, as well as by author and title. There are basically two ways to give subject access to research materials. Most card catalogs and some electronic catalogs use a controlled vocabulary, drawing their subject headings from a predetermined list. Many different systems of headings exist, with the majority of U.S. research libraries using the *Library of Congress Subject Headings.* British research libraries are less standardized in their use of subject headings. Most, however, use some system resembling *LCSH* in structure, if not in the actual terms used.

The researcher is well advised to familiarize him or herself with the subject organization of the catalogs to be used in the course of a lengthy research project. This is especially true when working with either a new subject emphasis or with a rare book collection, archive, or local history collection. Though most subject heading systems attempt consistency, terminology inevitably changes over time. Most libraries will have materials on the same subject under several different headings, depending on when they were added to the collection. Few libraries have the resources to go back and recatalog every time cataloging rules or systems change, so a thorough examination of all possible headings is the only way to insure a comprehensive search. Scholars who have successfully found material under "ARCHITECTURE, VICTORIAN" may be surprised to find more recent material under the newer heading "VICTORIAN ARCHITECTURE."

Specialized collections offer a different problem in subject access. Many such collections have their own, unique headings systems, organized around the peculiar needs of their specialized subjects. Anyone assuming that material can be found under the same headings used in the research library may miss valuable sources. Often, these systems are not outlined for the users, and the only way in which to find what you want is through consultations with the librarian or curator responsible for the collection

Computer searching of bibliographic records has developed another type of subject searching only occasionally used in print indexes. Key word searching uses the vocabulary of the bibliographic record itself, and sometimes an abstract, to identify the subject of the material. An example will clarify the way this type of subject searching is used. Paula Gillett's book *Worlds of Art: Painters in Victorian Society* (New Brunswick, N.J.: Rutgers University Press, 1990) has five subjects assigned it by the Library of Congress catalogers:

"PAINTING, BRITISH," "PAINTING, VICTORIAN--GREAT BRITAIN," "FEMINISM AND ART--GREAT BRITAIN," "ART AND SOCIETY--GREAT BRITAIN," and "GREAT BRITAIN--CIVILIZATION--19TH CENTURY." A card catalog would give me five places to find this book by subject and only these five. Looking under "VICTORIAN ART" would yield nothing, though it is a legal *LCSH* subject heading. A catalog allowing key word searching would allow access to this title through a search by any word in the title of the book. You could therefore find it under "PAINTERS" but not "PAINTING;" under "VICTORIAN" but not under "19TH CENTURY." In some systems this type of searching is further refined by the use of key word in context searching. Key word in context ties words together in the search. In library catalogs, this feature is most commonly governed by the "field" you are searching. The author is one field, the title another, publication information another. If I cannot remember the exact title of Gillett's book but only the words "worlds" and "art," a key word in context search would allow me to tell the computer that I want to find books with these two words appearing in the title. This search would find the book I am looking for, *Worlds of Art;* it would also find *Art World* and any other title containing the words "art" and "worlds" in any combination.

This means of subject searching has the advantage of flexibility and is especially useful for new subjects not yet listed in standard subject listings. However, it also demands that all possible synonyms for a subject be tried and requires some amount of imagination in the searcher. The most powerful and flexible computer catalogs allow searching by both key word and controlled vocabulary.

Card Catalogs. The card catalog, though rapidly being replaced by catalogs in various electronic formats, is still an important form of access to major research collections. Even libraries with online systems for recent acquisitions often have a card catalog for older imprints.

Therefore it is still of some importance to understand the basic organization and filing rules of library card catalogs.

Card catalogs come in two basic types. The dictionary catalog is in one alphabet, with author, title, and subject cards interfiled. Some libraries separate their catalogs into two sections, one containing all of the subject cards and the other the author and title cards. A third catalog type, the shelf list, is usually confined to library staff use, but you may encounter it in archives or in documents libraries. This file lists books in the order in which they appear on the shelf, by call number or accession number. Libraries having a public shelf list will usually have catalogs or finding guides with author, title, and subject access points and the number under which the book is listed in the shelf list.

In most American libraries, filing within card catalogs follows the rules of the American Library Association. These rules are many, but for most uses, two basic principles will allow you to find what you need. The most basic rule is that filing is done word-by-word rather than letter-by-letter. This means that spaces within titles are meaningful for filing, with a blank space a kind of invisible letter coming before A. The difference between letter-by-letter filing and word-by-word filing is best seen by example:

Word by word	Letter by letter
I knew a phoenix	The idea of God
I never danced at the White House	I knew a phoenix
The idea of God	Indian miniature painting
Indian miniature painting	I never danced at the White House

Obviously the two methods of filing can yield vastly different results. Studies by librarians indicate that the most common reason for failure to find the desired material in the card catalog is the user's lack of familiarity with filing methods, and this simple rule causes the greatest number of problems.

The second rule is that cards are filed in the order author-subject-title when the same word is used on more than one type of card. This rule is especially important for those doing research on any subject that appears in the catalog as both a subject heading and a title or, in the case of authors, as an author of books, the subject of books, and the title of books. Again, the principle is clearest from example. The example below shows the filing order when dealing with books by and about Dickens. Subject headings are in all capitals and titles are italicized:

Dickens, Charles, 1812-1870
The complete works of Charles Dickens
Dickens, Charles, 1812-1870
American notes for general circulation
DICKENS, CHARLES, 1812-1870
Adrian, Arthur A.
Georgina Hogarth and the Dickens circle.
DICKENS, CHARLES, 1812-1870
Ford, George Harry
The Dickens critics
DICKENS, CHARLES, 1812-1870--CHARACTERS
Brewer, Luther
Leigh Hunt and Charles Dickens
Dickens, Frank
Dickens and the rhetoric of laughter

Other rules may influence the order of card files, so if you fail to find the materials you need, it is wise to ask to have your search double checked by a librarian.

Online catalogs. Online catalogs have not yet achieved the same degree of standardization found in card catalogs.

What is searchable, the commands operating the system, and the degree of user friendliness vary greatly among the many systems found in research libraries here and in the United Kingdom. However, a unifying format, not always apparent to the user, does underlie the many online catalog systems in use. This is the MARC record.

MARC (for MAchine Readable Cataloging) is the basis for storing and sharing bibliographic information in a standardized format. The MARC record uses numbered "fields" to identify the various types of information that can be included in the cataloging of the book. For example, the 100 field contains information about the author of a book when the author is a person or persons. The 110 field is the author field when the author is a corporation, institution, or organization. Each of these fields has subfields containing various types of additional information necessary to identifying the item. Computers use these fields to identify the area in a record they need to look at when retrieving information.

Variations in online catalogs are partially explained by which of these fields the system is programmed to read and how the fields are read. Some information is stored so that you can see it when you call up the cataloging record, but you cannot search for the record by that information. Place of publication, publisher, and subtitles are unsearchable fields in many systems. Most systems include author, title, and assigned subject headings as searchable fields.

The best way to approach the wide variety of computer catalogs is with a series of questions that will give you some idea of their capabilities. Nothing is more frustrating than trying to make a computer system do something that it cannot do. You will need to know the information for which it will search. Does it allow key word or controlled vocabulary searches or both? Can you modify a search after it has been done? Does it allow access of the library you are in? More and more research libraries are hooking into the online catalogs of other research libraries and giving their users access to their holdings.

Once you know what can be found through a given catalog, you can find out how. Commands vary greatly from one system to the next, but most modern systems given some kind of online assistance to the user. Electronic catalogs usually can be searched either through a menu or through command language, though systems that operate exclusively through one means or the other also exist. Menus give lists of possibilities and the user selects an item number to give a command to the system. Command language requires that the user know the language and abbreviations that are meaningful to the system. You might inquire whether menu searching makes available all the commands possible to the system. Many are designed so that only the most frequently used searches are available through menus; the lesser used, and sometimes more powerful, searches are accessible only through commands.

Bibliographies, Indexes, and Abstracts

The vast majority of library catalogs do not include detailed analyses of the contents of the books and periodicals in that catalog. You can find out from the catalog that a certain journal is owned by the library and what issues of that journal are held but not if a particular subject has been covered in an article. For this purpose, bibliographies, indexes, and abstracts are essential tools for the scholar who aims at completeness. These three types of sources have in common that they identify materials that might not be found through library catalogs and that they are commonly found in the reference departments of large libraries, but, in other respects, they are different in purpose, accessibility, and coverage. Therefore, they need to be approached and judged in different ways.

The two types of bibliography are the single volume bibliography and the serial bibliography. Single volume bibliographies are self-contained, one-time efforts to cover a subject. Supplements may appear as need and opportunity occur, but the original bibliography is complete at the time it is written. This format makes them suitable for specialized or highly focused subjects.

Serial bibliographies generally cover larger, broader topics because they are updated at regular intervals. Both kinds of bibliography vary greatly in comprehensiveness, purpose, and accuracy, so it is best to approach any such source critically. Be sure to read all introductory material before using the bibliographic information. If the bibliography is annotated, what is the purpose of the annotations? Are the annotations critical or descriptive? A good bibliography will be explicit in stating its selection criteria and scope. Note whether the compiler has actually seen all of the items listed in the bibliography. Many famous bibliographic "ghosts" have been created by bibliographers depending on word of mouth and not confirming the existence of all items.

Indexes analyze the contents of periodicals and books. Some offer only subject approaches. Others may include subject, author, and title. Arrangement may be by subject or alphabetic. Organization and subject classifications may vary greatly from index to index, so a quick scan of any introductory material is advisable when using a source for the first time. Most indexes have introductory material explaining the subject covered, the range of sources used, and any exclusions.   Be sure you understand the scope of any index you use. The most frequent reason that users fail to find the information they need when using indexes is that they are using the wrong index. Librarians are invaluable resources for making sure you are using the best index for your purpose. Their daily contact with these sources makes them aware of strengths and limitations that might not be apparent to users focusing on one subject.

Abstracts are often shelved with indexes in libraries and used in a similar way as access points for the contents of periodicals and books. However, abstracts are more than just indexes with content summaries. First, their arrangement is almost always topical, with a series of indexes to provide author, title, and additional subject access. This arrangement offers the advantages and disadvantages of topical arrangements in libraries. Browsing within a topic becomes possible and can often lead to unexpected finds; however, cross-disciplinary research takes more preparation and an understanding of the structure of the abstract, since materials on such topics may be widely scattered. Secondly, abstracts can be great timesavers. A good abstract can tell a researcher if an article is likely to be useful for a particular topic, whether a title is misleading or an accurate description of content, and can suggest other key words and subject headings for further research without requiring the time-consuming search for the actual book or periodical. Like indexes, abstracts usually contain introductory material describing scope and arrangement, and it is important to be familiar with this material before beginning research in the source.

More and more serial bibliographies, indexes, and abstracts are appearing in the form of machine-readable datafiles or MRDFs. These databases are accessible in various ways. The two formats most often found in research libraries are the online database, delivered through several commercial services, and the CD-ROM, a laser-readable disc that can be searched in ways similar to online files. These products vary greatly in their degree of user friendliness. Some require such a degree of expertise that they are best searched by someone trained in using that database or database provider. Most research libraries offer some form of mediated searching, where a librarian or other specialist performs a search for you, often for a fee. More and more of the materials available through online systems and most of what is available on CD-ROM are user friendly to some degree and allow what is called "end-user searching." This means that the person who is going to use the information does his or her own search.

Perhaps the most useful aspect of MRDFs, including some online library catalogs, is the capability to do

Boolean searching. Search terms can be combined by the use of Boolean operators, *and*, *or*, and *not*, to widen, narrow, or refine a search. These words are used with the value they have in formal logic. Therefore, a search for Dickens *and* Thackeray will give a list on everything in the database that covers both of these authors together. A search for Dickens *or* Thackeray will yield all the books in the database on Dickens and all of the books or articles in the database on Thackery. Dickens *not* Thackeray will give everything that covers Dickens as long as it does not mention Thackeray. This capability is especially useful in cross-disciplinary research, because subjects not brought together in standard subject classifications can be combined.

Interlibrary Loan

No one library, even those at large research institutions, can supply every title needed for major research projects. As periodical prices increase and universities face shrinking budgets and increasing demands, the likelihood grows of finding that your home library does not have all that you need. Fortunately, interlibrary loan has increased in speed, efficiency, and coverage through the increased use of computer data-bases.

Though procedures differ from library to library, most libraries in the United States follow the National Interlibrary Loan Code of 1980. This code requires a full bibliographic citation for each request and a confirmation of this citation in some standard source. You will increase the speed with which your request is filled if you supply both the citation and the confirmation when you submit your request. Many of the sources listed in this bibliography are standard for this confirmation. The National Union Catalog (item 15), The British Library General Catalog of Printed Books (item 22), and The Union List of Serials in the United States and Canada and its supplements (item 14) are dependable sources widely used and trusted by libraries.

If you have access to either OCLC or RLIN (item 678), they are often the best sources for confirmation of

21

your citation. Both systems have interlibrary loan subsystems, and one or both of them are used by most research libraries in the United States. The presence of a listing in these databases indicates that the item is in the collection of some library belonging to the system and that it may be available through the system. Do not, however, take either database as the last word on the holdings of U.S. libraries. Both are weak on older imprints. If you are looking for a Victorian title, you may find the print catalogs of more use.

If the materials you wish to borrow through interlibrary loan are little-used, part of a major microform collection, or part of an expensive set, your ILL department may request the materials through The Center for Research Libraries. CRL is a corporation established by university and special libraries to acquire and lend research materials to supplement the holdings of its members. Its speed of response to requests is rapid and the terms of its loans are generous. A general acquaintance with the nature of its holdings can be a valuable resource when you are seeking a location for certain kinds of research sources. CRL publishes an annual handbook describing the nature of its collections. The handbook can be obtained from: The Center for Research Libraries; 6050 South Kenwood Avenue; Chicago, Ill., 60637.

Part II:

The Tools of Research

GUIDES AND BIBLIOGRAPHIES

The following sources are basic to almost any kind of library research, with special relevance for the humanities and the social sciences. For those who are uncomfortable or unfamiliar with research, the first two titles are useful basic guides to the process.

1. Barzun, Jacques, and Henry F. Graff. *The Modern Researcher*. 4th ed. San Diego: Harcourt Brace Jovanovich, 1985.

This unique guide to research combines information on research methods, on evaluation of sources and information, and on writing expository prose. The authors are historians, and examples are drawn from historical research, but the advice given can be used by almost anyone from the humanities or the social sciences. This edition adds to earlier editions materials on the use of word processors, data banks, and other computers.

2. Stevens, Rolland E., and Linda C. Smith. *Reference Work in the University Library*. Littleton, Colo.: Libraries Unlimited, 1986.

This volume is intended for instructional use in library schools. It is, however, of use to the non-librarian researcher for its description of the research strategies implied in various fields and for its exemplary annotations on various reference sources.

Most guides to research both list sources and suggest the most effective ways these sources might be used. The following guides cover a number of fields and a wide variety of reference sources. They are especially useful for their evaluations of reference materials. Researchers at all levels can use them as a guide to specific sources. They discuss matters of organization, scope, coverage, and quality of information.

3. Cheney, Frances Neel, and Wiley J. Williams. *Fundamental Reference Sources.* 2nd ed. Chicago: American Library Association, 1980.

This book is a standard source of information about basic, general reference tools. Entries include annotations indicating scope, organization, and type of information included.

4. Walford, A.J., ed. *Walford's Guide to Reference Material.* 4th ed. London: The Library Association, 1980-1987. v. 1. Science and Technology; v. 2. Social and Historical Sciences, Philosophy and Religion; v. 3. Generalities, Languages, the Arts, and Literature.

This guide is aimed at librarians and researchers. Annotations are critical and compare works on related or similar subjects. Emphasis is on English-language material, though coverage is international. This source is useful in identifing important bibliographies appearing in periodicals or as parts of books. A standard source.

5. Sable, Martin H. *Research Guides to the Humanities, Social Sciences, Sciences and Technology: Annotated Bibliography of Guides to Library Resources and Usage, Arranged by Subject or Discipline of Coverage.* Ann Arbor: Pierian Press, 1986.
This list of guides is a useful source for those seeking research guidance in a particular discipline. Entries include information on the purpose, authority, arrangement, scope, index, special features, and sources of review. Guides published from 1950 to 1986 are discussed, with the guides from the '50s discussed only if they are historically valuable or if nothing newer on the subject has been issued. Excellent beginning point for research in an unfamiliar area. Title and author indexes.

6. Kaplan, Fred, ed. *The Reader's Adviser: A Layman's Guide to Literature.* 13th ed. New York: Bowker, 1986.
Vol. 1: The Best in American and British Fiction, Poetry, Essays, Literary Biography, Bibliography, and Reference. Fred Kaplan, ed.
Vol. 2: The Best in American and British Drama and World Literature in English Translation. Maurice Charney, ed.
Vol. 3: The Best in General Reference Literature, the Social Sciences, History, and the Arts. Paula T. Kaufman, ed.
Vol. 4: The Best in the Literature of Philosophy and World Religions. William L. Reese, ed.
Vol. 5: The Best in the Literature of Science, Technology, and Medicine. Paul T. Durbin, ed.
This set identifies major research tools on a wide range of subjects. It should, however, be used with caution, since it lists only in-print sources. Though it is a good beginning source for those having little or no knowledge of a research field, more advanced scholars will want information with more historical depth. Organization varies from volume to volume, according to discipline.

7. Sheehy, Eugene P., ed. *Guide to Reference Books*. 10th
    ed. Chicago: American Library Association, 1986.
This volume is the definitive guide to American reference
works in all subjects and to foreign works commonly used
in American libraries. Organization is topical, with title
and author index. Entries include full bibliographic
information and descriptive notes.

UNION LISTS, CATALOGS, AND GUIDES TO COLLECTIONS

This section covers resources for identifying and locating collections on particular subjects and copies of specific books and periodicals. Confirming a bibliographic citation and finding a location for it is a time-consuming and often frustrating task. Online databases, such as OCLC and RLIN (see item 678), have simplified this work to some extent, but older titles often are not included in these sources. Research including Victorian sources is still tied to printed catalogs and bibliographies. Experienced scholars often have one favorite source for this type of information. For Victorian scholars, this source has long been the The British Library General Catalogue of Printed Books (item 22). As it grows, the Nineteenth Century Short Title Catalogue (item 11) may become of greater importance for this function. Whichever of these titles you choose to use as a first source, it is wise to be aware of the existence of other dependable lists, since no one catalog or bibliography will contain everything a scholar may want. Subject access to titles and collections presents a different problem. Several of the sources in this section are devoted to identifying major subject specializations in British and American libraries and so are an important resource at the beginning of a research project.

Publishing Records and Short-Title Catalogs

8. *English Catalogue of Books: Books Issued in the United Kingdom of Great Britain and Ireland.* London: Publisher varies: S. Low, 1864-1901; 1901-1965. Volume covering 1801-36, published in 1914, includes authors and keyword titles in one alphabet. 1835-1865 is numbered volume 1.

This title was the standard English trade list during its period of publication. It is fairly complete for books coming from the main centers of publication but is less good for provincial publications. Information included varies. Arrangement is in one alphabet, with author, title, and keyword entries, except from 1837 to 1889, when the subject entries were in separate index volumes.

9. *Cumulative Book Index.* New York: Wilson, 1928- .

The eleven monthly issues of this publishing record are cumulated quarterly, with an annual cumulation of the quarterlies. It serves as a single-alphabet subject, author, and title index to English-language books published throughout the world. Online and CD-ROM coverage are available through Wilsonline from the beginning of 1982.

10. *British National Bibliography.* London: British Library, Bibliographic Services Division, 1950- . Quarterly, the fourth issue being the annual cumulation.

"The objects of the *British National Bibliography* are to list new works published in the British Isles, to describe each work in detail and to give the subject matter of each work as precisely as possible" (Preface). Each yearly volume is in three parts: a subject section arranged by the Dewey Decimal System, an alphabetic section, and a subject index.

11. *Nineteenth Century Short Title Catalogue: Extracted from the Catalogues of the Bodleian Library, the British Library, the Library of Trinity College, Dublin, the National Library of Scotland, and the University Libraries of Cambridge and Newcastle.* Newcastle-upon-Tyne: Avero, 1984. Series I, 1801-1815, 5 volumes. Series II; Phase I, 1816-1870. 5 vols.

This project will eventually cover English-language books printed between 1801 and 1918. It should include all books published in Britain, its colonies, and the United States, and all books in English wherever published, and all translations from English. The first series, based on the holdings of the libraries listed in the subtitle, covers the period 1801-1815. It consists of five volumes. The second series covers 1816-1870 and will consist of 50 volumes; the third series will cover 1871-1918. As the introduction warns us, the texts themselves have not been examined. This is a listing of library holdings according to their catalogs. Inconsistencies of entry therefore exist, but extensive cross-references have done much to remedy problems. A subject index based on the Dewey Decimal Classification and an imprint index are included.

American Libraries

12. *American Library Resources: A Bibliographical Guide.* Chicago: American Library Association, 1951. 1st supplement, 1950-60, 1962; supplement, 1960-70, 1972; supplement, 1970-80, 1981.
These volumes list libraries with major holdings in specialized subjects. They include listings for these libraries of all published library catalogs, all checklists of specialized collections, calendars of manuscripts and archives, guides to individual libraries and their holdings, directories of libraries, union lists of periodicals, newspapers, and other serials, and any other published library guides useful to the scholar. All types of libraries are included. Arrangement is by broad subject field. Indexed.

13. *Directory of Special Libraries and Information Centers.* Detroit: Gale, 1963- .
This directory lists special and research libraries, archives, information centers, computer-based information systems, and other specialized collections in the United States, Canada, and, for large specialized systems, in other countries. The United States and Canada are treated together, with all other countries in a separate section. Arrangement within sections is alphabetical by the name of the library or its organization. Entries list address, phone, staff, subjects, holdings, services, and publications. Subject access can be gained in two ways. The directory has a subject index, and a separate set, *Subject Directory of Special Libraries and Information Centers,* (4 vols. Detroit: Gale, 1975-) gives the information in the main directory in classified listings. These volumes, each devoted to a different subject area, are indexed by title, alternate name, and detailed subject.

14. *Union List of Serials in Libraries of the United States and Canada..* 3rd ed. N. Y.: Wilson, 1965. 5 vols.
These volumes are the basic list of serials holdings in the libraries of the United States and Canada. Each entry gives a bibliographic description and a list of libraries with their holdings. This edition lists holdings through 1949. From 1950 on, periodicals are listed in *New Serials Titles* (Washington, D.C.: Library of Congress, 1953-). This title is issued in eight issues a year, with quarterly and annual cumulations. Cumulations exist for 1950-70 in four volumes, 1971-75 in two volumes, 1976-80 in two volumes, 1981-85 in six volumes, and 1986-88 in five volumes. A general subject classification is available through *New Serial Titles, Classed Subject Arrangement* (Washington: Library of Congress, 1955-) and *New Serial Titles, 1950-1970, Subject Guide* (New York: Bowker, 1975).

15. *The National Union Catalog, Pre-1956 Imprints: A Cumulative Author List Representing Library of Congress Printed Cards and Titles Reported by Other American Libraries.* London: Mansell, 1968-80. 685 vols.
These volumes list books, pamphlets, maps, atlases, and music in the Library of Congress and in major research collections throughout the United States and Canada. The set was continued by a supplement (London: Mansell, 1980-81, v. 686-754). Later acquisitions are covered in the *National Union Catalog, 1956 through 1967* (Totowa, N.J.: Rowman and Littlefield, 1970-72, 125 vols.), with annual supplements. These in turn cumulate quinquennially. In 1983 microfiche replaced paper. Access is through the main entry, usually author. Other access points are provided by the *Library of Congress Catalog. Books. Subject.* (Ann Arbor: Edwards, 1955) and its successor *U.S. Library of Congress. Subject Catalog.* This title ceased with the annual cumulation for 1982 and was replaced by the microfiche edition.

Machine-retrievable access for newer Library of Congress records is available through several sources. DIALOG offers file 426, LC-MARC— Books, and Wilsonline offers LCM-Library of Congress MARC Books File starting with 1977. These data files contain Library of Congress records for single books, but not for periodicals, newspapers, and serials, cataloged since 1968. OCLC and RLIN are also adding Library of Congress records to their databases. For more information on these systems, see item 678.

16. *Subject Collections: A Guide to Special Book Collections and Subject Emphases as Reported by University, College, Public, and Special Libraries and Museums in the United States and Canada.* Compiled by Lee Ash. 5th ed. Revised and enlarged. New York: Bowker, 1978.

The title describes the contents. Organization is by subjects based on the *Library of Congress Subject Headings* and then alphabetically by abbreviated state name. Arrangement is then by city followed by the name of the library. Though the book is the standard guide to special collections, it would be much more useful if some indexing were provided, including institutions listed. Increased use of cross reference has made subject searching easier in this edition. "See also" references would be a further improvement.

17. *The Main Catalog of the Library of Congress, 1890-1980.* New York: Saur, 1984-1989.

This microfiche edition of the main catalog of the Library of Congress reproduces 24.1 million cards giving LC holdings from 1890 to 1980, when the Library ceased putting entries in the card catalog and went completely to computer records. Cards include basic bibliographic information, though format differs depending on period. Arrangement is alphabetical by main entry.

British Libraries

18. *Libraries, Museums and Art Galleries Year Book: Incorporating the Librarians' Guide.* Cambridge: James Clarke & Co., 1897- .
This guide lists public libraries under the names of local authorities and special libraries, museums and art galleries, and stately homes under the names of towns. Entries include hours, admission policies, and scope of collections. Indexed by institution, subject, and special collections.

19. *British Union-Catalogue of Periodicals: A Record of the Periodicals of the World, From the Seventeenth Century to the Present Day, in British Libraries.* London: Butterworths Scientific Publications, 1955- . Supplements.
The first four volumes of this set appeared in 1955-58. A supplement was published in 1962, the *British Union-Catalogue of Scientific Periodicals.* This catalog now appears quarterly, with annual cumulations into two volumes, one general and one scientific. Each issue includes a list of New Periodical Titles, Index of Sponsoring Bodies, and Index of Library Symbols. Each entry includes a list of libraries in the United Kingdom holding that title.

20. *Catalogue of the Colonial Office Library.* Boston: G.K. Hall, 1969-72.

This catalog lists books, pamphlets, reports, official publications, periodicals, and articles in the Colonial Office Library. Imprint dates begin with the middle of the seventeenth century. Material on "all aspects of the organization of development of those countries which form or have formed part of the Commonwealth both before and after independence" (Preface) is included. The catalog is in two parts: material acquired before 1950, and a post-1950 catalog. The first supplement covers material acquired between 1963-67, and the second covers 1964-71, both having author/title and classified sections.

21. Roberts, Stephen, Alan Cooper, and Lesley Gilder. *Research Libraries and Collections in the United Kingdom.* London: Clive Bingley; Hamden, Conn.: Linnet Books, 1978.

This book gives an overview of research libraries and collections in the United Kingdom. The first section is a list of guides to libraries and collections; the second is a discussion of sources for archive and manuscript materials. "The inventory" forms the main part of the book, a listing of libraries, divided by kind of library (National and Public, University), then listed alphabetically by the official name. Entries include information on name of the parent institution, address and telephone number, historical information, subject coverage, statistics on holdings, special collections, arrangement, catalogs, admissions policy, hours, services, publications, and a list of publications describing the library and its collections. Useful in identifying places to pursue research.

22. The British Library General Catalogue of Printed
Books to 1975. London: Clive Bingley, 1979.
Supplements: London: Saur, 1976-1982, 1983;
1982-1985, 1986.

These volumes replace the *General Catalogue of Printed
Books* of the British Museum and list the more than eight
and a half million volumes of the British Library. Items
are listed under main entry and some cross references are
supplied. The amount of information in an entry varies
according to when the book was originally cataloged.

Subject access to the titles in this catalog is available
through *The British Library General Subject Catalogue*
(title and publisher vary). This index began with *Subject
Index of the Modern Works Added to the Library, 1881-
1900* (London, 1902-03, 3 v.). It has been updated
periodically: 1901-05, 1906-10, 1911-15, 1916-20,
1921-25, 1926-30, 1931-35, 1936-40, 1941-45,
1946-50, 1956-60. Subject headings tend to be general,
and no table of headings is given. The most recent subject
index is *The British Library General Subject Catalogue*,
covering 1975-1985 in 75 volumes.

Several machine-retrievable sources are also
available for British Library records. The *Catalogue* to
1975 in now available in a CD-ROM. These discs are
searchable in novice and expert formats, expert being
command driven, novice menu driven. Records are
searchable by author, title, keyword, subject, date,
imprint, place of publication, and bibliographical
information. Newer records are being added to both the
RLIN and the OCLC databases (see item 678).

23. Downs, Robert B. *British and Irish Library Resources: A Bibliographical Guide.* 2nd ed. New York: Mansell, 1981.
Title of 1st ed.: *British Library Resources.*
This guide attempts to list all published library catalogs, all checklists of specialized collections, calendars of manuscripts and archives, exhibition catalogs, articles describing library collections, guides to libraries and their holdings, directories of libraries, union lists of periodicals, newspapers, and other serials, and any other guides to libraries in the United Kingdom and Ireland. Because of the inclusion of union lists, holdings for libraries outside the British Isles also appear, but the author makes no attempt to be comprehensive on this non-British material. The lists are hierarchical, with general heading (Literature, Medicine) subdivided by specific fields. It is particularly strong on local history; the "History" section contains the division "British Local History," and this section is divided by place names. Research on individual persons is aided by the section "Individual Bibliography, Biography, and Criticism." An "Author/Compiler/Editor Index" and a "Subject Index" complete this well-organized source.

24. Codlin, Ellen M., ed. *Aslib Directory of Information Sources in the United Kingdom.* 5th ed. 2 vols. London: Aslib, 1982.
This directory is an alphabetic listing of British libraries. Entries list organization represented, place within a system, name changes, address, subject coverage, information services available, special collections, and publications. Subject index.

25. Williams, Moelwyn I., ed. *A Directory of Rare Book and Special Collections in the United Kingdom and the Republic of Ireland.* Edited for the Rare Book Group of the Library Association. London: Library Association, 1985.

This directory lists rare book collections throughout the United Kingdom and Ireland. Arrangement is geographical and then alphabetic. Entries include information on the library's address, telephone number, hours of opening, conditions of admission, research facilities, and a brief history. Collection descriptions include origin and history, size, summary of contents and subject fields. Information on catalogs and other published references to the collections have been included in many cases. Indexed.

26. Owen, Dolores B. *Guide to Genealogical Resources in the British Isles.* Metuchen, N.J.: Scarecrow, 1989.

This directory is organized in several sections. The main section is an alphabetical list by location of repositories of genealogical information. Other sections list special information on these repositories, such as credentials and holidays, a list of institutions arranged alphabetically by name, genealogical associations, town maps, a list of institutions by county, and a subject index. This subject index presents some access problems. Since it lists "individuals, families, estates, collections, and places not found in the name of the institution nor the town under which it is located," it is really only a partial subject list. Therefore, all lists must be scanned for key words if you wish a complete subject survey of the contents. Coverage is good and it is useful as the only up-to-date guide on this subject.

MANUSCRIPTS, ARCHIVES, AND UNPUBLISHED SOURCES

27. *The National Catalog of Manuscript Collections.*
Washington, D.C.: Library of Congress, 1959- .
Annual. Publisher varies.
This catalog gives reproductions of catalog cards for manuscript collections throughout the United States. Entries list number of items, description, scope and content, location, terms of access, finding tools, and availability of copies. Arrangement is alphabetical by collection name, most being personal papers. Indexes list names, places, subjects, and named historical periods. From 1959 to 1979, indexes were published at odd intervals, 1959-62, v. 3; 1963-66 in 1966 volume; 1967-69 in 1969 volume; 1970-74 in 1974 volume. In 1975, indexes were issued in separate volumes and cumulated annually, then quinquennially. Starting in 1988, an *Index to Personal Names* (Alexandria, Va.: Chadwyck-Healey, 1988. 2 vols) was published. All personal and family names are brought together in one alphabet, with a reference to the full catalog.

28.   Hepworth, Philip. *Archives and Manuscripts in Libraries.* 2nd ed. London: The Library Association, 1964.

This pamphlet is an informative introduction to archive and manuscript collections in Great Britain. The section "Catalogues and Guides to Manuscripts in Libraries" is still useful, especially for its list by geographic location of catalogues and guides to specific collections.

29.   Storey, Richard, and Lionel Madden. *Primary Sources for Victorian Studies: A Guide to the Location and Use of Unpublished Materials.* London: Phillimore, 1977.

This guide is directed to those starting primary-source research in Victorian studies. The emphasis is on archives and repositories in Great Britain, but some attention is given to finding material outside of Britain. Indexed by subject. A useful overview for the beginning researcher.

30.   Emmison, F.G. *Introduction to Archives.* London: Phillimore, 1978.

This pamphlet introduces the reader to archival material, with emphasis on English and Welsh local history. Very basic and general.

31.   British Library. Department of Manuscripts. *Index of Manuscripts in the British Library.* Cambridge: Chadwyck-Healey, 1984.

This alphabetical index replaces over 30 catalogs and indexes. All collections acquired up to 1950 are covered. It allows the user to identify individual items, the collection to which it belongs, its number within the collection, and its folio or article number. This last number can be used for ordering photocopies and microfilms. New cross references aid in finding main entries.

32. United States. Historical Publications and Records Commission. *Directory of Archives and Manuscript Repositories in the United States.* 2nd ed. Phoenix: Oryx Press, 1988.
This directory describes U.S. manuscript repositories and archives. Organized by state, then by city, entries list name, address, telephone number, days and hours of operation, user fees, access policies, copying facilities, acquisitions policy, holdings, nature of holdings, and guides to the collections. Indexed by subject and repositories.

33. Foster, Janet, and Julia Shepard. *British Archives: A Guide to Archive Resources in the United Kingdom.* 2nd ed. New York: Stockton Press, 1989.
This book is an alphabetical listing, by location, of all types of archival material. Entries list parent organization, address, telephone, person to whom enquiries should be addressed, hours, historical background, major collections, and facilities available to users. Includes bibliography, index to collections and key subject word index.

GUIDES TO MUSEUMS AND COLLECTIONS

Museums are valuable research centers for scholars interested in visual arts or in material culture. The following sources describe British and American collections covering the Victorian period. These guides date rapidly on such matters as opening hours and policies. Most, however, give information on arranging research privileges.

34. Standing Committee on Museums and Galleries. *Guide to London Museums and Galleries.* London: HMSO, 1974.

This guide describes the collections in major museums and galleries in London. Individual entries run from 1 1/2 to 10 pages and give an overview and highlights of collections. The 1974 edition covers 22 museums and galleries in depth and gives brief descriptions of other museums.

35. *Museums Yearbook: Including a Directory of Museums and Galleries of the British Isles.* London: The Museums Association, 1976- . Former title: *Museums Calendar.* 1957-75.
This annual publication includes a directory of museums and art galleries in Britain and the Republic of Ireland. Entries give address, governing body, admission charges, accessibility for disabled, public facilities, report if published, catalog if published, opening hours, attendance figures, and staff listing. Other information on museums, such as membership in associations and commissions, is also listed in the directory.

36. *American Museum Guides. Fine Arts.* Consultant editor Tom L. Freudenheim. New York: Macmillan, 1983.
This guide to American museums offers information on hours, admissions, publications, research facilities, and collections of the major U.S. art museums.

37. Abse, Joan. *The Art Galleries of Britain and Ireland: A Guide to Their Collections.* Revised ed. London: Robson Books, 1985.
This guide reviews the permanent collections of the public art galleries of Britain and Ireland. Arranged alphabetically by city, the entries list gallery name, location, phone number, and opening hours. This information is followed by an essay, ranging in length from one paragraph to several pages. The essays give brief histories of the listed galleries and overviews of their collections. An excellent index helps locate the works of specific artists.

GENERAL REFERENCE SOURCES

The almanacs, bibliographies of bibliographies, encyclopedias, indexes, and statistical handbooks listed here, though general, are rich sources of information on the Victorians. Many date back to the nineteenth century and so are primary sources of information on the knowledge and attitudes of the Victorian period. Modern encyclopedias and almanacs offer overviews of our knowledge of this period. Bibliographies of bibliographies and indexes are excellent starting points for research requiring secondary sources. The following items were selected for their special strength in Victorian subjects or their value in providing current information on this area.

Almanacs

38. *Annual Register: A Review of Public Events at Home and Abroad.* London: Longmans, Green, 1758- .
    Title varies: *Annual Register,* 1758-1953; current title, *Annual Register of World Events.*
This annual covers, through both narrative and lists, the major events each year. The contents vary over the years, but some subjects are generally covered, the historical surveys of Britain and other nations being one constant. The 1874 volume, for example, contains sections on: English history, Foreign history, Retrospect of literature, Arts and science, Chronicle of remarkable occurrences, Obituary of eminent persons, and Remarkable trials.

39. *An Almanack.* London: Whitaker, 1869- .
Whitaker's provides statistical and other types of factual information for the late Victorian period. The index (in the front of each volume) gives detailed subject access to the contents.

Bibliographies

40. *Bulletin of Bibliography.* Westwood, Mass.: Faxon, 1897- . Quarterly.
This periodical includes bibliographies on all subjects. The bibliographies are indexed in many standard indexes, including *Bibliographic Index* (entry 41) and *Victorian Studies* (entry 73).

41. *Bibliographic Index: A Cumulative Bibliography of Bibliographies.* New York: Wilson, 1937- .
This serial lists by subject bibliographies having 50 or more citations. Bibliographies appearing in books, pamphlets, and periodicals are included, as well as separately published works. It appears in April and August, with cumulation in December. The online database from Wilsonline begins with November 1984 and is updated twice weekly. A CD-ROM is forthcoming.

42. Besterman, Theodore. *World Bibliography of Bibliographies: And of Bibliographical Catalogues, Calendars, Abstracts, Digests, Indexes, and the Like.* 4th ed. Lausanne: Societas Bibliographica, 1965-66. 5 vols.
These volumes list by subject bibliographies on all subjects, inclusive to 1963. This monumental work includes extensive cross references, listings of subdivisions for subjects classified by country, and an exhaustive index. The basic five volumes include about 117,000 bibliographies.
   This work is continued and updated by Alice F. Toomey in *A World Bibliography of Bibliographies, 1964-1974: A List of Works Represented by Library of Congress Printed Catalog Cards; A Decennial Supplement of Bibliographies* (Totowa, N.J.: Rowman and Littlefield, 1977. 2 vols.). Toomey follows Besterman's organization.

43. Brewer, Annie M., ed., with the assistance of Amy F.
    Lucas. *Indexes, Abstracts, and Digests: A Classified Bibliography Reproduced from Library of Congress Cards Arranged According to the Library of Congress Classification System.* Detroit: Gale, 1982.
This bibliography consists of reproductions of Library of Congress catalog cards for indexes, abstracts, and digests on all subjects on which LC has holdings. Arrangement is by Library of Congress classification. A key word index helps those unfamiliar with the system. No other indexing.

Dictionaries and One-Volume Encyclopedias

44. Kent, William, ed. *An Encyclopaedia of London.* New York: Macmillan, 1951.
This book is an alphabetically arranged list of places and topics in and of London. Its age is some drawback, making such entries as "Restaurants" outdated. More historical entries are still valuable, however. The entries in this title are longer and on broader topics than those in Weinreb and Hibbert's *The London Encyclopaedia* (see item 46).

45. Isaacs, Alan, and Jennifer Monk, eds. *The Cambridge Illustrated Dictionary of British Heritage.* Cambridge: Cambridge University Press, 1986.
This handy dictionary defines and discusses a broad range of words and phrases that might be unfamiliar to those beginning Victorian studies. You can look up "almshouses," "baronet," "City of London," "Ruskin College," and many other terms here.

46. Weinreb, Ben, and Christopher Hibbert, eds. *The London Encyclopaedia.* Bethesda, Maryland: Adler & Adler, 1986.

This encyclopedia is a guide both to historical and present-day London. Two indexes, one to people, one general, provide guidance to finding specific subjects in more general articles. Identifying the concrete, physical aspects of the London scene is the special strength of this title.

47. *Oxford English Dictionary.* Prepared by J.A. Simpson and E.S.C. Weiner. 2nd ed. 20 vols. Oxford: Clarendon Press, 1989.

The 2nd edition of the OED brings together the contents of the original 12 volumes, published in 1933, and the four supplements appearing between 1972 and 1986. In addition, about 5,000 new words have been added. Long the essential source for English linguistic history, its usefulness is further enhanced by the the CD-ROM version now available. It allows all of the information in an entry to be searched, giving access to information by date, quoted author, definition, and many more fields. At this time, the CD is limited to the contents of the 1933 edition.

Encyclopedia Sets

48. *Encyclopaedia Britannica.* 1st-14th eds. Chicago: Encylopaedia Britannica, 1768- . Place of publication varies.

The *Encylopaedia Britannica* is for many *the* English-language encyclopedia, especially in its late nineteenth and early twentieth century editions. Up until the 14th edition, appearing in 1929, it differed from other encyclopedias in that it featured monographs on large subjects written by specialists but did not include separate treatment of smaller topics or information on living persons.

Britannica's greatest accomplishment was the 1875-1889 9th edition, under the editorship of William Robert Smith. The contributors to this edition read like a who's who of distinguished Victorian scholars, including Matthew Arnold, Walter Besant, Austin Dobson, Andrew Lang, William Michael Rossetti, and other famous names. For subjects not requiring recent information, this edition is still a standard source. The 11th edition, though more popular in style, is of similar quality.

The 14th edition in 1929 introduced shorter, more specific articles. A continuous revision policy was then instituted, and new edition numbers were not assigned until 1974, when *The New Encyclopaedia Britannica* (15th ed. Chicago: Encyclopaedia Britannica. 30 v.) was introduced. This edition changed the structure of the *Britannica,* combining the monographic articles of the pre-1929 editions with shorter articles. The section containing the longer articles is called the *Macropaedia;* shorter articles appear in the *Micropaedia.* The *Propaedia* is a one-volume outline of knowledge. Originally, indexing was included in the *Micropaedia.* In 1985, separate indexing was added to the set, the *Micropaedia* was expanded, and the *Macropaedia* reduced. The result is better access to the dependable and informative articles.

49. *Chamber's Encyclopaedia.* London: International Learning Systems, 1859- . Publisher varies.
The first edition of this famous encyclopedia was published in 520 weekly parts between 1859 and 1868. Over one hundred contributors worked on this edition, and it is a treasure of Victorian knowledge and opinions, as is the 1888-92 edition. The more recent editions are true to their Victorian origins and remain a useful source for quick but thorough information on things Victorian.

Statistics

50. Great Britain. Board of Trade. *Statistical Abstract for the United Kingdom.* v. 1-83, 1840-1923. London: Printed for Her Majesty's Stationery Office by Eyre and Spottiswoode. Repr. Vadez: Kraus Reprint LTD., 1965.
Each volume of this abstract contains statistics for the previous fifteen years. Subjects covered vary slightly from volume to volume, with the emphasis on demographic and commercial information.

51. Mitchell, B.R., with the collaboration of Phyllis Deane. *Abstract of British Historical Statistics.* Cambridge: Cambridge University Press, 1962.
Mitchell, B.R. and H.G. Jones. *Second Abstract of British Historical Statistics.* Cambridge: Cambridge University Press, 1971.
These abstracts contain demographic and economic statistics from 1199 on, with emphasis on the eighteenth and nineteenth centuries. Because many times and subjects are covered, information is general. The first abstract regularizes the information in the *Statistical Abstract of the United Kingdom* (entry 50). The *Second's* chief purpose is to extend the first volume's cutoff date of 1938 to 1965 or 1966, with some a few pre-1938 figures.

Periodicals

A number of directories list currently published periodicals. Each has a slightly different format and emphasis and, therefore, different uses. The four most commonly encountered in libraries are:

52. *Gale Directory of Publications: An Annual Guide to Newspapers, Magazines, Journals, and Related Publications.* 2 vols. Detroit: Gale, 1880- . Title varies; most recently *Ayer Directory of Publications.*

This directory lists American and Canadian newspapers and periodicals by the place of publication. It gives brief information on the city of publication, followed by entries for each title. Entries give name of publication, frequency, character or political leaning, date of foundation, size of column or page, subscription price, circulation figures, and names of editors and publisher. This is the only one of these directories to include information on newspapers.

53. *Ulrich's International Periodicals Directory.* 3 vols. New York: Bowker, 1932- . Biennial, with annual cumulation. Title varies; frequency varies.

This classified directory covers periodicals from all over the world. Entries include, as appropriate, title, subtitle, sponsoring group, date of origin, frequency, price, editors, publisher, place of publication, annual and cumulative indexes. Its most useful feature is the listing of which indexing or abstracting service indexes a periodical.

Irregular Serials and Annuals: An International Directory covers publications appearing irregularly. The information from both titles and from *Ulrick's Update* can be searched on DIALOG database 480.

54. *The Standard Periodical Directory.* New York: Oxbridge Communications, 1964- .
This directory lists by broad subject areas United States and Canadian periodicals. Information includes name and address of publisher, editorial content and scope, year founded, frequency, subscription rate, circulation, and advertising rates.

55. *The Serials Directory: An International Reference Book.* 3 vols. Birmingham, Al.: Ebsco, 1986- .
This directory is the newest of the major listings of periodicals and so lacks the extensive backrun of annuals that are often useful to the scholar of the nineteenth century. It covers an international list of titles in four sections: Serials Listing, Alphabetical Title Listing, Ceased Title Listing, and ISSN Index.

Indexing to scholarly periodicals tends to follow discipline lines. Therefore, indexes to current periodicals will be discussed with other research tools for the disciplines. Earlier indexes were less subject-specific, however. The following indexes are guides to popular periodicals of the Victorian period. Retrospective indexes, such as the Wellesley Index to Victorian Periodicals, *are covered in the section on Victorian studies.*

56. Poole, William Frederick, and William I. Fletcher. *Poole's Index to Periodical Literature.* Gloucester, Mass.: Peter Smith. Vol. 1, revised ed., 1802-1881, 2 parts, 1963. 1st supplement, 1882-1886, 1938. 2nd supplement, 1887-1891, 1938. 3rd supplement, 1892-1896, 1938. 4th supplement, 1897-1901, 1938. 5th supplement, 1902-1906, 1938.

Poole's is a subject index to 479 English and American periodicals published between 1802 and 1906. Items lacking a non-fiction subject, such as stories, poems, and plays, are listed under the first word of the title not an article. Reviews of literary works are under the name of the author reviewed; reviews of non-fiction are listed under the subject of the book.

C. Edward Wall's *Cumulative Author Index for Poole's Index to Periodical Literature, 1802-1906* (Ann Arbor, Mich.: The Pierian Press, 1971) lists Poole's authors alphabetically. Many of the author attributions in Poole's are inaccurate and no attempt at correction has been made here. Marion V. Bell and Jean C. Bacon alphabetized the periodical titles in the various volumes of Poole in *Poole's Index, Date, and Volume Key* (Chicago: Association of College and Research Libraries, 1957). Vinton A. Dearing's *Transfer Vectors for Poole's Index to Periodical Literature* (Los Angeles: Pison Press, 1967) lists the periodicals by abbreviation and gives the full title, dates indexed, and the volume number of Poole's indexing.

57. *Nineteenth Century Reader's Guide to Periodical Literature, 1890-1899, with Supplementary Indexing 1900-1922.* New York: Wilson, 1944.

This index analyzes 51 periodicals, 13 of which are British. Listings are by author, subject, and illustrator, with the emphasis on subject access. Some anonymous authors are identified.

Newspapers

Daily and weekly newspapers from major urban areas and the more occasional rural papers are useful for all areas of Victorian studies and of special importance to local history. The following lists can help the researcher establish when and where newspapers were published.

58. *The Times.* London. *Tercentenary Handlist of English and Welsh Newspapers, Magazines, and Reviews.* London: The Times, 1920.

This list begins with the year 1620 and goes through 1919. Section I covers the London and Suburban press, Section II the provincial press. Organization is by the date of the earliest copy which has been found for examination. Information includes number and date of the earliest issue, date of discontinuance if known, and, in some cases, printer, editor, distributor, and a reference to the library or collection in which the title can be found if it is other than the British Museum's general collection. It claims to be nearly exhaustive for the nineteenth century.

59. Toase, Charles A., ed. *Bibliography of British Newspapers.* London: British Library, 1975- . Vol. 1: Wiltshire, 1975. Vol. 2: Kent, 1982. Vol 3. Durham and Northumberland, 1982. Vol 4: Derbyshire, 1987. Vol. 5: 1987.

These bibliographies list newspapers in the covered areas from the earliest known to the present day. Sections begin with a chronological list of papers from or covering events in that area. Earliest and latest known years of publication are given in this list. The main section is an alphabetical list of newspapers, by their most recent title if still published, by first title if ceased. Each entry lists place of publication, locations of copies, and historical accounts of the paper, if such exist. Indexes of title and places.

Two press guides were published during the Victorian period. These guides gave different information at different periods, but, generally, they included information on the newspaper publishing trade and on the politics and policies of various newspapers.

60. *Newspaper Press Directory.* London: Benn Bros., 1846-1976. Reprint. Washington: Microcard Editions, 1968. Titles varies. No volumes issued 1848, 1849, 1850, 1852, 1853, 1855.

This guide covers British newspapers and an overview of the press in other countries. The first edition, listed the information to be included: "1. The leading features connected with the population, manufactures, trade, &c., of each newspaper district.— 2. Title, price, day, and place of publication of each newspaper.— 3. Its politics.— 4. The date of its establishment.— 5. The principal towns in what is considered its more especial local district.— 6. The particular interest it advocates, whether it is attached to the Church of England, or is the organ of a sect of Dissenters.— 7. The names of the proprietors and publishers.— 8. And whether the bookselling, stationery, or any business is carried on at the office."

61. *Willing's Press Guide.* London: Willing, 1874- . Annual.

Willing's is still published and is an essential guide to newspapers and periodicals of the British Isles. Since its emphasis has changed over the years, it is a good idea to become familiar with its range of coverage. At all times, it is an excellent source for information on ownership of newspapers and periodicals.

Though the suburban and provincial press are of great importance to the student of Victorian England, nothing can replace the Times *as the central source of news and the voice of the establishment press in Britain.*

62. *Palmer's Index to the "Times" Newspaper, 1790-
    June 1941.* London: Palmer, 1868-1943.
    Reprint. New York: Kraus, 1965.
This quarterly subject index to the *Times* lacks annual
cumulations, and its erratic indexing makes *Palmer's*
difficult to use. Headings used vary from issue to issue, but
one consistent element is the heading "Deaths," a useful
source of biographical information.

*For information on publications about the British
newspaper press, consult*

63. Linton, David and Ray Boston, eds. *The Newspaper
    Press in Britain: An Annotated Bibliography.*
    London: Mansell Publishing Limited, 1987.
This bibliography covers publication about the newspaper
press in Great Britain and Northern Ireland from 1476 to
1986. Arrangement is alphabetical by author, with
annotations on the author, the content of the work, and an
evaluation. It also includes two appendixes: a chronology of
British newspaper history and a location of useful
archives. Index by title, subjects, and joint authors.

Dissertations

*English-language dissertations from the United States,
Canada, and Great Britain are well indexed. Online
databases have further improved the accessibility of
bibliographic information on dissertations. The following
indexes and abstracts, used together, will give a
comprehensive listing of the available dissertation
literature.*

American Doctoral Dissertations

64. *Dissertation Abstracts International: Abstracts of Dissertation Available on Microfilm or as Xerographic Reproductions.* Ann Arbor: University Microfilms, 1938- . Monthly, with annual cumulated author index. Title varies.
These volumes are a listing with abstracts of doctoral dissertations submitted to University Microfilms International. Varying numbers of universities have worked with UMI over the years, so the number of college and universities covered varies. Arrangement is by subject field. Each issue includes a subject and author index. See item 66 for information on further indexing and online versions.

65. *American Doctoral Dissertations.* Compiled for the Association of Research Libraries. Ann Arbor: University Microfilms, 1957- . Annual. Title varies.
This annual lists dissertations for which doctoral degrees were granted in the United States. It includes a more complete list than does DAI but does not include abstracts.

66. *Comprehensive Dissertation Index.* Ann Arbor: Xerox University Microfilms, 1973- .
This annual list of American dissertations is compiled from various sources, including *DAI* (item 64), *American Dissertation Index,* and Library of Congress records. A convenient and comprehensive source, it includes listings by subject, by key word, and an author index. Entries give the original source and the UMI order number, when it exists. *DAI, Comprehensive Dissertation Index,* and *Masters Abstracts* (item 67) are searchable online through *Dissertations Abstracts Online.* This database is available through both DIALOG and BRS. It is updated monthly and goes back to 1861. Abstracts are available for dissertations added since 1980. It is also available in a CD-ROM version.

American Masters Theses

67. *Masters Abstracts.* Ann Arbor: University Microfilms
    International, 1962- .
This abstract is published quarterly. Its arrangement and
the information given is similar to that in *DAI* (item 64).
It is not, however, nearly as comprehensive as *DAI.*

British Dissertations and Theses

68. *Index to Theses Accepted for Higher Degrees in the
    Universities of Great Britain and Ireland.* London:
    Aslib, 1950- . Annual. Title varies.
This index to British and Irish theses is organized by broad
subject, with indexes by author and by more specific
subjects drawn from key words in the dissertation titles.
Entries include abstracts.

MULTIDISCIPLINARY REFERENCE SOURCES

Multidisciplinary and cross-disciplinary areas of study, such as Victorian studies, have in recent years increasingly occupied scholarly attention. Because these subjects do not follow traditional information paths and because they are relatively new, research in these fields presents some unique problems. Drawing on many disciplines, they require a breadth of knowledge not easily acquired by a specialist. The following sources focus on these multidisciplinary fields and attempt to lead the researcher to both new resources specific to the emerging field and resources from various disciplines useful in cross-disciplinary studies. In this section, I have included only sources dealing with more than one discipline. Reference sources dealing with these topics within disciplines, such as women's studies in literature, are included with the books on that discipline.

Victorian Studies

Research Guides

69. Madden, Lionel. *How to Find Out About the Victorian Period.* Oxford: Pergamon Press, 1970.
This exhaustive guide covers general reference sources necessary to all researchers and sources specifically on the Victorian period. It is divided by broad subject field and sample pages from major sources are included. Though it was published before the current flood of reference sources on the period appeared, it is still invaluable as a guide to research methods and sources, especially for information on Victorian reference tools.

Encyclopedias

70. Mitchell, Sally, ed. *Victorian Britain: An Encyclopedia.* New York: Garland, 1988.
This one-volume encyclopedia contains signed articles on "persons, events, institutions, topics, groups, and artifacts in Great Britain between 1837 and 1901" (Preface). Each essay includes a brief bibliography on the discussed subject. The contents include a chronology, bibliography on general research materials, and a subject index.

Serials

71. Houghton, Walter E., ed. *The Wellesley Index to Victorian Periodicals, 1824-1900.* 5 vols. Toronto: University of Toronto Press; London: Routledge and Kegan Paul, 1979-1989.
The first four volumes of this set index major Victorian periodicals, with a full tabular listing of each title's contents. The fifth volume, the epitome and index, completes the project. The index lists by author's name or pseudonym all contributions to the analyzed journals, with the exception of poetry. The final volume is, however, more than a simple index. Biographical notes to each entry give as complete a name as is known, dates and occupation for each author. This index, with the identification of pseudonymous authors in the four initial volumes, offers a rich and invaluable source for the study of the periodical literature of Victorian Britain.

72. Fulton, Richard D., and Charles Michael Colee, eds. *Union List of Victorian Serials.* New York: Garland, 1985.
This list identifies libraries in the United States and Canada holding runs of selected Victorian serial publications. Based on the list of periodicals in volume 3 of the *New Cambridge Bibliography of English Literature* plus about 100 titles in science and technology, it is alphabetical by serial title. Dates held are included. No effort has been made to standardize conflicting bibliographical information but the conflicts are noted so that the researcher is aware of the need for caution in using the information.

Annual Bibliographies

73. "Victorian Bibliography." *Victorian Studies.* Annual.
    v. 1, 1957-.
The "Victorian Bibliography," appearing each summer
issue in *Victorian Studies,* is a continuation of an earlier
annual bibliography published in *Modern Philology.* It is
prepared by a committee of experts and covers books
published in the previous year having a bearing on the
Victorian period. Selected items from earlier years,
missed in previous bibliographies, are also included. The
bibliography is divided by broad subject categories. Each
entry includes bibliographic information and, where
possible, a listing of reviews that have appeared on that
item. Of central importance to both specialized subject
research and more general work on the period.

74. *Annual Bibliography of Victorian Studies.* Edmonton:
    LITIR Database, 1976- .
This bibliography lists the year's work, primarily in
English, on Victorian studies. Sections include: General and
Reference Works; Fine Arts; Philosophy and Religion;
History; Social Sciences; Science and Technology; and
Language and Literature, with listings for individual
authors. It includes listings of selected reviews for some
entries. Indexing is by subject, author, title, and
reviewer. *A Comprehensive Bibliography of Victorian
Studies* (Vol. 1, 1970-74; Vol. 2, 1975-79; Vol. 3,
1980-84. Edmonton: LITIR Database, 1984) expands and
corrects the annual volumes and omits the review listings.
Further correction and expansion occur in *Cumulative
Bibliography of Victorian Studies* (2 vols. Edmonton: LITIR
Databases, 1988-). Volume One of this set covers the
classified listings, and Volume Two contains the indexes. In
all of these sets, subject indexing is limited to literary
authors and the general emphasis is literary, with smaller
sections on other fields.

75. Wolff, Michael, John S. North, and Dorothy Deering. *The Waterloo Directory of Victorian Periodicals, 1824-1900.* Phase I. Sponsored by The Research Society for Victorian Periodicals and Waterloo Computing in the Humanities. Waterloo, Ont.: The University of Waterloo, 1977.
This listing of newspapers and periodicals published in England, Ireland, Scotland, and Wales between 1824 and 1900 is the handlist for a series of more comprehensive directories. The first of these, *Waterloo Directory of Irish Newspapers and Periodicals,1800 to 1900* (item 78) appeared in 1986. Volumes on Scotland and England are due to appear soon. Arrangement in Phase I is alphabetical by earliest know title. Since entries are drawn from the *Union List of Serials* (item 14), the *British Union-Catalogue of Periodicals* (item 19), and the *Tercentenary Handlist of English and Welsh Newspapers, Magazines, and Reviews* (item 58) and copies of the described periodicals have not been examined for this phase, inconsistencies and omissions occur. Useful, but to be used with caution.

Single-Volume Bibliographies

76. Altholz, Joseph L. *Victorian England: 1837-1901.* Cambridge: Cambridge University Press, 1970.
This bibliography covers the history of Victorian England. Divided by type of history, including science and technology, religion, and the fine arts, arrangement within sections is by type of publication and then alphabetical by author. Indexed by authors, editors, and translators. It is directed to the advanced student and scholar.

National Studies

Ireland

77. Eager, Alan R. *A Guide to Irish Bibliographical Material: Being a Bibliography of Irish Bibliographies and Sources of Information.* 2nd revised and enlarged edition. Westport, Conn.: Greenwood Press, 1980.

This bibliography cites bibliographies, reference works, and periodical and newspaper articles on all aspects of Ireland and its culture. Arrangement is by Dewey Decimal Classification, with author and subject indexes.

78. North, John S., ed. *The Waterloo Directory of Irish Newspapers and Periodicals, 1800-1900: Phase II.* Waterloo, Ont.: North Waterloo Academic Press, 1986.

This directory, phase two of the Waterloo project (see item 75), lists newspapers and periodicals from Ireland "in all fields, published from daily to annual frequency." It includes over 3900 titles and cross reference, with subtitles, title changes, dates, series, editors, printers, price, subjects, departments, illustrations, indexing, mergers, and locations of copies. Indexed by subject, by place, and by personal name.

79. Lester, Dee Gee, comp. *Irish Research: A Guide to Collections in North American, Ireland, and Great Britain.* New York: Greenwood, 1987.

This guide lists collections in Irish Studies. Arrangement is geographical; Canada, the United States, Ireland, and Great Britain are covered. Includes information on contents of collections and conditions of use. Subject index.

Scotland

80. Black, George F. *A List of Works Relating to Scotland.* New York: The New York Public Library, 1916. This catalog lists works on Scotland owned by the New York Public Library at the beginning of the century. Many of the listed works are Victorian. Arrangement is by subject area. Indexed.

81. Hancock, P.D. *A Bibliography of Works Relating to Scotland, 1916-1950.* Edinburgh: The University Press, 1959. 2 vols. This unannotated, topically arranged bibliography lists books published between 1916 and 1950 on all aspects of Scottish studies. The first volume covers general materials and regional information. The second volume is by broad subject area.

82. Fraser, Kenneth C. *Bibliography of the Scottish National Movement, 1844-1973.* Dollar, Scotland: Douglas S. Mack, 1976. This bibliography lists books and pamphlets of eight pages or more issued by Scottish Nationalist bodies, periodicals with a large amount of information on the Nationalist Movement, and books containing "a substantial section on Scottish Nationalism" (Introduction). Entries are not annotated. Indexed by author, periodical title, and organization. Arrangement is topical, including a section on the history of the movement. No access by date or period.

83. Grant, Eric G., comp. *Scotland.* Santa Barbara: Clio Press, 1982. This bibliography covers all aspects of Scottish life and culture. Arrangement is topical, with an author, title, and subject index. Entries include descriptive annotations. Useful for basic materials.

Women's Studies

Research Guides

84. Williamson, Jane. *New Feminist Scholarship: A Guide to Bibliographies.* Old Westbury, N.Y.: The Feminist Press, 1979.
This guide to bibliographies on feminist studies has sections on history, literature, and art and music. It covers both serial and one volume bibliographies.

85. Barrow, Margaret. *Women, 1870-1928: A Select Guide to Printed and Archival Sources in the United Kingdom.* New York: Garland, 1981.
This bibliographic guide covers a wide range of material on both women and British society in the late nineteenth and early twentieth centuries. The central focus is the social and economic position of women. The guide is divided into four parts: archives, printed works, non-book material, and libraries and record offices. Each part is then divided topically. A detailed subject/name index is included, as well as an author/title index. It gathers together much hard-to-find information. An update would be useful.

86. Searing, Susan E. *Introduction to Library Research in Women's Studies.* Boulder: Westview Press, 1985.
This guide presents techniques and sources for research in women's studies. It is useful both for its look at specific research tools and for an approach to interdisciplinary study. Author, title, and subject indexes.

Periodicals

87. Palmegiano, E.M. *Women and British Periodicals,
    1832-1867: A Bibliography.* New York: Garland,
    1976.
This bibliography lists British women's periodicals and
articles on women in British periodicals for the period
1832-1867. The introduction covers images and
characteristics of various groups and classes of women as
seen in the periodicals of this period. Also published as
Victorian Periodicals Newsletter (9, 1976).

88. Danky, James P., ed. *Women's Periodicals and
    Newspapers from the 18th Century to 1981: A
    Union List of the Holdings of Madison, Wisconsin
    Libraries.* Boston: G.K. Hall, 1982.
This list includes nearly 1500 periodicals and newspapers
relating to women. Arrangement is alphabetical, with
information on title, year began and ceased, frequency,
subscription rates for currently published titles, current
editor and address, ISSN, OCLC number, LC card number,
number of pages in latest issue, size of latest issue,
whether title contains drawings, photographs, advertising,
or color material, where title is indexed, if available in
microform, previous editors, subject focus, and holdings
at various libraries. This bibliography provides
dependable bibliographic and access information on many
women's periodicals of Victorian Britain.

89. Doughan, David, and Denise Sanchez. *Feminist Periodicals, 1855-1984: An Annotated Critical Bibliography of British, Irish, Commonwealth, and International Titles.* Washington Square, N.Y.: New York University Press, 1987.

This guide to feminist periodicals includes mainly British titles. Arrangement is chronological. Each entry includes title as found on the title page, variant titles, editor, publisher, frequency, date of first and last issue, location, and availability in microform. Indexed by name and title, by subject, and by chronology.

Bibliographies

90. Helsinger, Elizabeth, Robin Lauterbach Sheets, and William Veeder. *The Woman Question: Society and Literature in Britain and America, 1837-1883.* 3 vols. New York: Garland, 1983.

These three volumes are a series of bibliographic essays on the literature of "the woman question." Volume 1 covers *Defining Voices,* the works of those early writers who stated the issues that would be debated throughout the century; volume 2 covers *Social Issues,* and volume three *Literary Issues.* The essays go far beyond merely describing the works listed; they are important works in themselves on the position and perception of women in Victorian Britain and America. Each volume separately indexed.

Diaries and Autobiographies

91. Matthews, William, comp. *British Autobiographies: An Annotated Bibliography of British Autobiographies Published or Written Before 1951.* Berkeley: University of California Press, 1955.
This bibliography is the standard reference work on British autobiography, covering from the Middle Ages to 1951. Arrangement is alphabetical by author, with an excellent subject index. Brief contents notes.

92. Batts, John Stuart. *British Manuscript Diaries of the Nineteenth Century: An Annotated Listing.* Totowa, N.J.: Rowman, 1976.
This book lists unpublished diaries of the Victorian period. It is arranged by year of the earliest volume, listing author, in some cases birth and death dates, and identification by place or profession, dates of diaries, contents, and location of diary. List of diaries with no date, and indexes of diarists and subjects.

93. Hacket, Nan. *XIX Century British Working-Class Autobiographies: An Annotated Bibliography.* New York: AMS Press, 1985.
This bibliography covers published autobiographies by manual laborers, describing life in Britain from 1800 to 1900. Some were written during that period, some later. An introduction tracing the general history of working-class autobiography precedes the bibliography. Arrangement is chronological. Each entry includes author, title, publisher, locale, writer's occupation, and an annotation on the content and style of the book. Indexed by author and by locales, occupations, and major events.

94. Huff, Cynthia. *British Women's Diaries: A Descriptive Bibliography of Selected Nineteenth-Century Women's Manuscript Diaries.* New York: AMS Press, 1985.
This bibliography lists unpublished diaries by women. Arrangement is by social class, then chronological by earliest date of entry. Annotations describe and evaluate content and style. Indexes by diarist and subject. This item used with Batts (item 93), give excellent coverage of the manuscript diaries of the Victorian period.

95. Havlice, Patricia Pate. *And So To Bed: A Bibliography of Diaries Published in English.* Metuchen: N.J.: Scarecrow, 1987.
The diaries here were all published as books, chapters in books, or journal articles; no manuscript material is included. Arrangement is by author, with some brief identification, citation, and some notes. Author, title, subject index. Access to particluar periods is difficult, since no indexing by period, country, or date is provided.

96. Cline, Cheryl. *Women's Diaries, Journals, and Letters: An Annotated Bibliography.* New York: Garland, 1989.
This bibliography contains information on the personal writings of women. It lists alphabetically by author diaries, journals, and letters, indexing them by profession or significant characteristic and by subject. Short chapters on other bibliographies, critical works, and anthologies give selected secondary sources. Despite its completeness and the thorough research that went into it, design and indexing problems limit its usefulness. Indexing categories are often overly general, and no subheadings are used for large categories. Index references are by page rather than citation number, so you must guess which citation on a page is the one you are seeking. No listing of included authors and no running heads are used to make finding a specific author easier.

97. Davis, Gwenn, and Beverly A. Joyce. comps. *Personal Writings by Women to 1900: A Bibliography of American and British Writers.* London: Mansell, 1989.
This bibliography lists published diaries, journals, letters, memoirs, travel literature, and autobiographies published before 1900. Arrangement is alphabetical, by author. Good cross-references lead from maiden and pen names to main entry. A chronological listing of names is included in an appendix and an index lists countries, professions, and events. Omissions of material that one would expect to find here and typographical errors mar this otherwise useful title.

98. Riddick, John F. comp. *Glimpses of India: An Annotated Bibliography of Published Personal Writings by Englishmen, 1583-1947.* Bibliographies and Indexes in World History 15. New York: Greenwood, 1989.
This bibliography lists 580 memoirs, autobiographies, collections of letters, diaries, journals, and travel narratives of the British in India. Arrangement is chronological, with three chapters, 1818-1857, 1857-1858, and 1858-1905, covering the Victorian period. Annotations are descriptive with brief evaluative comments. The chronological arrangement makes the bibliography useful for study of the period, but the lack of a subject index makes approach to a particular subject within the topic of the British in India difficult. Author index only.

Arts, Humanities, and Social Sciences

Many of following sources are not truly cross- or interdisciplinary in that they deal with sources observing the traditional discipline boundaries. They do, however, deal with more than one of these disciplines. They can therefore be used with profit by those looking for basic sources in unfamiliar fields, often the first step in beginning interdisciplinary research.

Research Guides

99. Webb, William H. and others. *Sources of Information in the Social Sciences: A Guide to the Literature.* 3rd. ed. Chicago: American Library Association, 1986.

This volume is the standard source for information on resources in all branches of the social sciences. Separate chapters cover general social science literature, history, geography, economics, and business, sociology, anthropology, psychology, education, and politics. Historical as well as contemporary information is given for all subjects. Valuable first source.

Indexes

100. *Essay and General Literature Index.* New York: H.W. Wilson, 1934- .
This index to English-language essay collections and anthologies emphasizes the humanities and social sciences. Subject and author are in one alphabet. Two issues a year are cumulated in the second issue, with a five year cumulation. Coverage is retrospective to 1900. Online coverage from Wilsonline begins with December 1985.

101. *British Humanities Index.* London: Library Association Publishing Ltd., 1963- .
This index started in 1915 under the title *Athenaeum Subject Index;* in 1919 the title changed to *Subject Index to Periodicals.* It appeared under its current title starting in 1963, and some of its contents went into another index, *British Technology Index* (see item 533). Over the years arrangement has varied. The 1915-16 volume was an alphabetical listing by subject and author. 1917 to 1919 was arranged by class, with an author index. 1920 to 1922 was also by class, but no author index was included. No index was published 1923 to 1925. In 1926, an alphabetical subject list with no author access was used and continued to 1961. From 1962 to the present, quarterly issues have been indexed by subject; annual cumulations have both subject and author sections. Subject headings and cross references are especially good in this index. (For example, see list of articles and of related headings under "Victorian Age" in any issue.)

102.   *Humanities Index.* New York: Wilson, 1974- .
This quarterly index lists the contents of periodicals in a broad range of humanities, including history. The quarterly issues cumulate annually. Title and coverage have varied. From 1970 to 1965, it was called *International Index* and covered the literature of both the social sciences and the humanities. From 1965 to 1974, the title was *Social Sciences and Humanities Index.* In 1974, the index was divided into the current two titles (see also item 104). The index is available through Wilsonline and on a CD-ROM from February 1984 on.

103.   *Social Sciences Index.* New York: Wilson, 1974- .
This quarterly index to periodicals on a broad range of social sciences is cumulated annually. From 1907 to 1965, it was known as *International Index;* from 1965 to 1974 as *Social Sciences and Humanities Index.* It is available online on Wilsonline starting from February 1984 and in a CD-ROM starting with 1983 indexing.

104.   *Arts and Humanities Citation Index.* Philadelphia: Institute for Scientific Information, 1977- .
This index is issued three times a year, with the last issue being cumulative for the year. The index has three main sections: Citation Index, Source Index, and Permuterm Subject Index. Also included are a Corporate Index and Guide and Journal lists. The primary use of the index is to find which authors are being cited in what sources. It can be searched by author cited, by source of citation, or by subject. The subject index is not strong. A useful feature is that citations are given for illustrations of works of art. Book reviews are also covered. The index is more flexible and searchable through Dialog database 439 or BRS file AHCI, from 1980 to present.

Bibliographies

105. *London Bibliography of the Social Sciences.* 4 vols.
     London: Mansell, 1931-32. Supplements, vol.
     5, 1934-. Publisher varies.
This bibliography is the most extensive subject bibliography on the social sciences. Arrangement is alphabetical by subject. The subheading "— Great Britain— History" is used with many headings ("Coal Mining— Great Britain— History"), as are period subdivisions (Economics— History— 19th century). Coverage is international and includes books, pamphlets, and documents. Extremely useful.

106. Gray, Richard A., with Dorothy Villmow, comps.
     Serial Bibliographies in the Humanities and Social Sciences. Ann Arbor: The Pierian Press, 1969.
This selective bibliography lists serial bibliographies, that is, any bibliography which "at the initial time of publication, is intended to be issued indefinitely at reasonably regular intervals." It is especially useful in identifying what the author call "concealed bibliographies," works appearing regularly in journals, as well as those published as separate books. It lists ceased as well as active titles.

Organization is based on the Dewey Decimal Classification System. The volume is extensively indexed by title, author, publisher, sponsor, subject, keyword-in-context, and selected characteristics. An extensive Introduction gives complete instructions for use. Though badly in need of an update, the book is valuable for its identification of hard-to-find research sources.

Government Publications

In the past, government documents and archives were essential to all types of historical research and extremely difficult to use. Though they have lost none of their importance, over the past twenty years they have become easier to use, thanks to the many excellent guides and indexes that have been added to the classic finding aids such as Hansard. The following titles provide access to published and unpublished documents of the British government and to the unpublished papers of those involved in governing. Her Majesty's Stationery Office has been especially assiduous in producing guides to both official and unofficial records having to do with the government of nineteenth century Britain. The beginning researcher would be well advised to become thoroughly familiar with the guides to the particular class of document or papers in which he or she is interested. They are great time-savers and provide access to otherwise hidden treasures.

Research Guides

107. Giuseppi, M.S. *A Guide to the Manuscripts Preserved in the Public Record Office.* 2 vols. London: HMSO, 1923-24.
Many of the documents produced by departments of the British government have been preserved in the Public Record Office by an 1838 Act of Parliament. These volumes define what is considered a "record" and list some of the important documents preserved. Arrangement is by department of origin. An introduction to this guide was written in 1949 and reprinted in 1953 (Public Records Office. *Guide to the Public Records; Part I, Introductory.* London: HMSO, 1949; Repr. 1953). (See also item 144).

108. Bond, Maurice. *The Records of Parliament: A Guide for Genealogists and Local Historians.* Bridge Place, Canterbury, Phillimore, 1964.
This brief guide is an introduction to records of Parliament and gives sources for further access to these records. Good first source for newcomers to Parliamentary records.

109. Pugh, R.B. *The Records of the Colonial and Dominions Offices.* Public Record Office Handbooks, No. 3. London: HMSO, 1964.
This guide describes administrative arrangements for handling relationships with the countries of the Empire or Commonwealth, describes the records of the administrations, gives notes on the record classes.

110. Great Britain. Public Records Office. *The Records of the Foreign Office, 1782-1939.* Public Records Office Handbooks, No. 13. London: HMSO, 1969.
This guide introduces the records of the Foreign Office groups and related groups in the Public Records office. Part I is an administrative history of the Foreign Office between 1782 and 1939. Part II describes the records created by this administration; Part III gives four sample searches showing the various registration and record-keeping systems that have been used; and Part IV lists the classes in the Foreign Office group.

111. Bond, Maurice F. *Guide to the Records of Parliament.* London: HMSO, 1971.
This guide describes the records of both Houses of Parliament, all documents presented to the two houses or purchased by them, and papers accumulated in various Parliamentary and non-Parliamentary offices in the Palace of Westminster. The information covers records from the fifteenth century to 1970. Both manuscripts and published records are listed, with greatest attention to the manuscripts. Arrangement is by the provenance of the document and a subject index provides additional access.

112. Ford, Percy, and Grace Ford. *A Guide to Parliamentary Papers: What They Are; How to Find Them; How to Use Them.* 3rd ed. Shannon, Ireland: Irish University Press, 1972.
This guide is a useful introduction to the types and contents of parliamentary papers. Though more recent guides may give more in-depth information on certain aspects of these papers, none give a better overview. Invaluable for the first-time user of these papers.

113. Pemberton, John E. *British Official Publications.* 2nd rev. ed. Oxford: Pergamon Press, 1973.
This book describes the various types of British official publications. It also covers the indexes and catalogs to these publications. Chapter 8, "Parliamentary Debates," with its discussion of Hansard (see item 123) is especially useful to the Victorian scholar.

114. Emmison, F.G., and Irvine Gray. *County Records.* Revised. London: The Historical Association, 1973.
This guide introduces the reader to the Quarter Session records of England and Wales. Sections include: Records of the Courts of Quarter Sessions and of Petty Sessions; Other County Records; Topography and Genealogy in County Records; and Local and National History in County Records. Appendices give lists of Printed Catalogues and Transcripts of County Records and The County Record Office and the Student.

115. Office of Population Census and Surveys. General Register Office. Edinburgh. *Guide to Census Reports: Great Britain, 1801-1966.* London: HMSO, 1977.
This guide to the census reports is a valuable aid to research. It lists the reports, describes the development of the census reports, gives the questions asked at the census, provides guidance to finding certain categories of information, and discusses the uses of census information.

116. Rodgers, Frank. *A Guide to British Government Publications.* New York: Wilson, 1980.
This guide covers publications issued by British government departments and related agencies. The emphasis is on current publications, but the information used to find current materials can also be used to locate earlier work by the discussed agency. Useful for its comprehensive coverage of departments.

117. Bond, Maurice F. *A Short Guide to the Records of Parliament.* 3rd ed. revised. London: House of Lords Record Office, 1980.
This guide describes the history of the Parliamentary archives, the types of materials available in them, and the care of the documents by the Office. Information is basic and well explained.

118. Richard, Stephen, comp. *Directory of British Official Publications: A Guide to Sources.* London: Mansell, 1981.
This guide identifies "the full range of publishing by official organizations and sources of supply." Its main use, therefore, is in identifying and procuring current British government publications, including those of various historical agencies, libraries, and museums.

119. Cox, Jane, and Timothy Padfield. *Tracing your Ancestors in the Public Record Office.* 3rd ed. Public Record Office Handbooks, No. 19. London: HMSO, 1984.
This handbook introduces the beginner to the use of the Public Records Office. Its purpose is to guide the genealogist, but it could be used by the social or local historian. Information on types of records, censuses, wills, finding information on various groups of people (soldiers, Manxmen, emigrants, clergy), and other sources of information are presented simply and clearly.

120.   Jones, David Lewis. *Debates and Proceedings of the British Parliaments: A Guide to Printed Sources.* London: HMSO, 1986.

This guide lists printed sources for the proceedings of the Parliaments at Westminster, the Irish Parliament, the Parliamentary Institutions in Northern Ireland, and the Scottish Parliament. Within each of these sections, entries are chronological. Entries are annotated. Indexes by author and important titles.

121.   Higgs, Edward. *Making Sense of the Census: The Manuscript Returns for England and Wales, 1801-1901.* Public Record Office Handbooks, No. 23. London: HMSO, 1989.

This guide offers information on the history, structure, interpretation of, and reference sources on nineteenth century census-taking. It is valuable for the researcher in this period because it covers the manuscript returns. Earlier guides have dealt mainly with the published reports. The censuses of England and Wales are covered; Scotland, Ireland, and the colonies are not. Important starting point for those new to census materials.

Accessions Lists

122.   Great Britain. The Royal Commission of Historical Manuscripts. *Accessions to Repositories and Reports Added to the National Register of Archives.* London: HMSO, 1957- . Title varies.

This list provides concise descriptions of important or unusual accessions to British repositories each year.

Indexes and Catalogs to Public Documents

123. Great Britain. Parliament. *Parliamentary Debates.* Vol. 1-41 (1803-1820); n.s. Vol 1-25 (1820-1830); 3rd ser. Vol 1-356 (1830-1890/91); 4th ser. Vol 1-199 (1892-1908). London. Publisher varies.

This series of indexes is generally cited as Hansard, after its original compiler. A general index covers the first and second series (London: Baldwin, 1834). The remaining series must be approached through the sessional indexes. The indexes list debates both under the names of speakers and under the subject of their addresses. However, the indexes are made difficult to use by a lack of cross references. Entries in the index are to column numbers, with volume numbers in brackets. The four series covering the Victorian period are not official transcripts and are not complete. For subject access, the Irish University Press reprints (item 139) and the next item supplement the assistance supplied by Hansard.

124. Great Britain. Parliament. House of Commons. *General Index to the Reports of Select Committees Printed by Order of the House of Commons, 1801-1852.* London: House of Commons, 1853.

This index is another of the early subject listings of the papers of the House of Commons. A brief descriptions of the document is included with information on session, page number, volume number and m.s. page number.

125.   Great Britain. Parliament. House of Commons.
       General Index to the Bills, Reports, Estimates,
       Accounts, and Papers, Printed by Order of the
       House of Commons and to the Papers Presented
       by Command 1852/53-1868/69. London:
       House of Commons, 1870. Also 1870-
       1879/79 (1880).
This index lists by subject the command papers and other
reports printed by order of the House of Commons between
1852 and 1869. Entries give a brief description of the
contents of the item and cite the session, the paper
number, the volume and the m.s. page. A volume covering
1870-1878/79 followed. The predecessors to this index
were the *General Index to the Bills, 1801-1852* (1853)
and the *General Index to the Accounts and Papers, Reports*
of Commissioners, Estimates, &c, 1801-1852 (1853).

126.   *List of Parliamentary Papers for Sale From Session*
       1836 to Session 1872. London: n.p., 1874.
This sales list of government publications serves as a non-
exhaustive list of materials available from this period.
Arrangement is in two sections: by date and alphabetical.
Identification by brief title.

127.   Adams, Margaret I., John Ewing, and James Munro.
       Guide to the Principal Parliamentary Papers
       Relating to the Dominions, 1812-1911.
       Edinburgh and London: Oliver and Boyd, 1913.
This guide to Parliamentary Papers relating to the
Dominions gives session, volume, number of the paper, and
pages of the volume. Arrangement is by countries, with a
personal name and subject index.

128. *HMSO Annual Catalogue.* N.P.: HMSO Books, 1922-. This catalog lists all items published by HMSO during a given year (excluding Statutory Instruments and Statutory Rules of Northern Ireland) and items published by British organizations for whom HMSO acts as sales agent. The first section lists Parliamentary publications by series number; the second section lists publications by corporate body responsible for their production.

The annual catalog is the cumulation of a series of catalogs to British government publication, These include: *Daily List, Monthly Catalogue, Annual Catalogue, International Organizations Annual Catalogue, Statutory Instruments,* the quarterly *Committee Reports Published by HMSO Indexed by Chairman, HMSO in Print on Microfiche, Weekly List, Sectional Lists,* and *Consolidated Indexes.* The *Consolidated Indexes* is a five-year cumulation of the indexes of the *Annual Catalogue.*

129. Cole, Arthur Harrison. *Finding List of British Royal Commission Reports: 1860 to 1935.* Cambridge, Mass.: Harvard University Press, 1935.
This list of Royal Commission reports produced between 1860 and 1835 is organized by broad topics. A Preface discusses Royal Commissions, their composition and purpose.

130. Temperly, Harold, and Lillian M. Penson. *A Century of Diplomatic Blue Books, 1814-1914.* Cambridge: University Press, 1938.
This book gives "a list of the titles of Foreign Office Blue Books from Castlereagh to Grey," and indicates the dates on which they came before Parliament. It includes much valuable information about these books, including, in some cases, omissions and mutilations.

131.   Cole, Arthur Harrison. *A Finding-List of Royal Commission Reports in the British Dominions.* Cambridge, Mass.: Harvard University Press, 1939.

This list covers overseas members of the British Commonwealth or the old British self-governing colonies for ten years before the present forms of government were introduced for each nation. Records as early as 1877 are included for some areas. Arrangement is by country, then by subject classifications.

132.   Jones, T.I. Jeffreys. *Acts of Parliament Concerning Wales, 1714-1901.* Cardiff: University of Wales Press, 1959.

This is a topically arranged listing of the long titles of Parliamentary Acts "that either deal exclusively with Wales or give special regard to places or persons in Wales." Acts are arranged chronologically within subject sections; an index by proper names eases access.

133.   Powell, W.R. *Local History From Blue Books: A Select List of the Sessional Papers of the House of Commons.* Helps for Students of History. London: The Historical Society, 1962.

This basic guide to the use of the Sessional Papers of Commons is designed to help the student of local history find and evaluate this material. It describes the types and arrangement of sessional papers, discusses the reliability of the information in them, and tells how to cite the papers.

134. Great Britain. Public Records Office. *List of Cabinet Papers, 1880-1914.* Public Records Office Handbooks, No. 4. London: HMSO, 1964.

This list covers the papers dealing "with matters on which Cabinet Ministers thought it worth while to arrange for a printed memorandum to be circulated to their colleagues." The papers, therefore, cover a wide variety of subjects. The list is in chronological order. Volume numbers lead to copies of the papers in the Public Record Office. Date and authorship are given when available and a list of cabinet ministers signing or initialling the papers is included.

135. *List of Colonial Office Confidential Print to 1916.* Public Record Office Handbooks, No. 8. London: HMSO, 1965.

This handbook lists "over 2,500 printed papers in which selected correspondence, memoranda and other documents were copied for internal use in the Colonial Office or, in some cases, for circulation to the Cabinet." This collection is particularly important for the study of British colonial activities in the late Victorian period, because some of the original correspondence for the period 1874 to 1890 has been destroyed. The list is arranged in eight sections according to the region, with a miscellaneous section at the end. Entries describe, briefly, the subject of the document, give the date, a physical description, and the reference number for finding material in the Search Room of the Public Record Office.

136. Ford, Percy, and Grace Ford. *Select List of British Parliamentary Papers, 1833-1899.* Shannon, Ireland: Irish University Press, 1969.

This guide is arranged by subject, with an alphabetical index. It "includes the report and all other material issued by committees and commissions or similar bodies of investigation into economic, social and constitutional questions, and matters of law and administration." The list is based on the House of Commons papers and includes only those Lords' papers communicated to Commons.

137. Lo Hui-Min. *Foreign Office Confidential Papers Relating to China and Her Neighbouring Countries, 1840-1914; With an Additional List 1915-1937.* The Hague: Mouton, 1969.
This list of Confidential Papers is arranged numerically. Classification numbers assigned by the Foreign Office and the Public Records Office are given in brackets. Titles are given as they appear on the Print. A useful guide to esoteric material and to study of the Empire in the Far East.

138. *Catalogue of Parliamentary Papers 1801-1900: With a Few of Earlier Date.* Together with Supplement I: 1901-1910; and Supplement II: 1911-1920. London: King & Sons, 1904-22. Repr.: New York: Burt Franklin, 1972.
This catalog is an annotated subject index to important Parliamentary papers. Arrangement is alphabetical, by subject, with some cross references.

139. *Checklist of British Parliamentary Papers in the Irish University Press 1000-Volume Series, 1801-1899.* Shannon, Ireland: Irish University Press, 1972.
The Irish University Press reprint program for British Parliamentary papers is a boon to those seeking material on selected subjects in the Parliamentary Papers. Editors have selected from the chronological volumes papers on the same subject and gathered them together. The 1,000 volumes of the set cover nineteenth-century papers in 32 subject areas. To increase ease of use, a series of bibliographic guides accompanies the set.

This checklist is the basic index to the IUP set. It is divided into three parts. Part 1 is a chronological list by session, allowing those who know which paper they want to find it in the subject set. Part 2 is a table of contents for the 1,000-volume set, arranged alphabetically by IUP subject classification. Part 3 contains a keyword title index and a chairman/author index. The bibliographic guides include several focusing on special subjects: children's employment, Canada, Australia and New Zealand are covered at book length, and a number of pamphlet-length guides cover many other topics. This set is an invaluable supplement to *Hansard* (see item 123).

140. Cobb, H.S., comp. *A Handlist of Articles in Periodicals and Other Serial Publications Relating to the History of Parliament.* House of Lords Record Office Supplementary Memorandum. London: House of Lords Record Office, 1973.

This handlist gathers citations to articles in all types of serial publications on the history of Parliament. It is in three sections: general histories of parliament; histories of one of the houses; and special aspects of Parliamentary history. Divided chronologically and by subject.

141. Great Britain. Parliament. House of Lords. *A General Index to the Sessional Papers Printed By Order of the House of Lords or Presented by Special Command.* Dobbsferry: Oceana, 1976. 1801 to 1859 (Session 1), Vol. 1, A-H; 1801-1859 (Session 1), Vol. 2, I-Z; 1859-1870; 1871-1884/5

This set indexes the sessional and command papers of Lords from 1801 to 1885. The main part is a reprint in facsimile of the index first published in 1860. The publishers have added a checklist of House of Lords Sessional papers, a guide to the publisher's microfilm edition of the House of Lords Sessional Papers, and a supplementary section for papers found only in the microfilm edition. The microfilm edition of the papers is available in 560 reels from Trans-Media Publishing.

142. *Catalogue of British Official Publications Not Published by HMSO.* Cambridge: Chadwyck Healey, 1981- . Bimonthly, with annual cumulations.

This catalog lists publications for organizations "financed or controlled completely or partially by the British Government" and not published by HMSO. Organization is by agency, with a subject index. Since over half of all British official publications are now issued outside of HMSO, this index provides valuable information on all subject areas. The index is also searchable online as DIALOG file 228, starting with 1980.

143. Richard, Stephen, comp. *British Government Publications: An Index to Chairmen of Committees and Commissions of Inquiry.* Vol. I: 1800-1899. London: The Library Association, 1982.
"This index covers committees of the House of Commons and the House of Lords, commissions of inquiry and selected reports by individuals to commissions and branches of government." Arrangement is by surname of authors and chairmen, with "see" references from titles and name variants. Citations to both the bound set of parliamentary papers and the Irish University Press reprint of the House of Commons sessional papers are given. Invaluable, both as a key to the work of particular persons and to reports known popularly by the names of their authors.

144. *Current Guide to the Contents of the Public Record Office.* Kew, P.R.O., 1983- .
The *Current Guide* replaces the *Guide to the Contents of the Public Records Office* (London: HMSO, 1963-1968), which was based on Giuseppi's *Guide to the Manuscripts Preserved in the Public Record Office* (item 107). It includes both additions made to classes included in the old guide and new record groups and classes added since 1968. Part I describes the history, organization, and function of the departments and courts for which the PRO includes records; Part II lists the nature and contents of each class; Part III indexes persons, places, subjects, and institutions. It is being updated regularly on microfiche.

145. Cockton, Peter. *Subject Catalogue of the House of Commons Parliamentary Papers, 1801-1900.* Cambridge: Chadwyck-Healey, 1988.
This five volume set is the only source providing subject access to the entire set of nineteenth century Parliamentary papers. It covers every Parliamentary document for this period. Arrangement is by nineteen subject groups, with each subject subdivided into several sections. Papers are arranged under keyword or description within each section; an alphabetical index of the descriptors is in the final volume. Within each subject, papers are separated by type of document and then listed chronologically and in paper number order. Papers in series are listed by their first publication date. Entries are keyed to both the printed edition and the Chadwyck-Healey microfiche edition. An invaluable and unique tool for a difficult research area.

Private Papers

146. *Papers of British Cabinet Ministers, 1782-1900.* Guides to Sources for British History. London: HMSO, 1982.
This guide to the papers of nineteenth century cabinet ministers revises and extends John Brooke's 1968 *The Prime Ministers' Papers 1801-1902* (London: HMSO). Coverage starts with Rockingham's second administration, March 1782. It ends with March 1900. It includes papers, both political and personal, that remained in the hands of a former Cabinet minister or his secretary at the time of his death. Entries include name and titles, birth and death dates, offices held, with dates, brief account of career, description of contents of papers, and current holders of the papers. Index of institutions. Brooke's volume is still of use for the access points not provided in the newer guide: list of correspondents, list of printed materials, and a list of manuscript collections.

147. *Private Papers of British Diplomats, 1782-1900.* The Royal Commission on Historical Manuscripts. London: HMSO, 1985.

This volume is the result of a survey of "the surviving private papers of British diplomats, consuls, and Foreign Office officials in post between 1782 and the beginning of the present century." Included are drafts or copies of dispatches, diplomatic notes, personal journals, memoranda, and private letters exchanged between diplomats and their superiors. Private papers are included for all not covered in *Papers of British Cabinet Ministers, 1782-1900* (see item 146). Arrangement is alphabetical by personal name. Entries give name of diplomat, dates, description of career, nature of documents, and holder of material. Index by the institution holding the described materials.

148. Great Britain. The Royal Commission on Historical Manuscripts. *Private Papers of British Colonial Governors, 1782-1900.* Guides to Sources for British History. London: HMSO, 1986.

This guide describes the private papers of British colonial governors and senior officials of the Colonial Office. British India and British North American Canada are not included. Since the papers are private, dispatches and other official papers of the Colonial Office records are excluded. Papers are listed by author, with an index of institutions.

Locations

149. *Guide to the Location of Collections Described in the Reports and Calendars Series, 1870-1980.* Guides to Sources for British History. London: HMSO, 1982.
This publication is a location guide for collections described in the Reports and Calendars series. The Introduction discusses the confusing bibliographic history of this series. The body of the volume is an alphabetical list of collections with information on location and the number of the report in which they are described.

150. Great Britain. The Royal Commission on Historical Manuscripts. *Record Repositories in Great Britain: A Geographical Directory.* 8th ed. London: HMSO, 1987.
This guide lists by location the record repositories for national records and local records, and universities, college, special libraries, and departments financed by the central government. The directory gives address, hours, access, copying facilities, and depository status.

REFERENCE SOURCES FOR VARIOUS DISCIPLINES

The following sources are arranged by traditional academic disciplines. Some are general, dealing with all aspects of the field, and some are specifically concerned with the nineteenth century or the Victorian period. The general sources have been chosen for their strength in introducing their subjects to those from other fields or those new to advanced academic research, with an emphasis on British aspects of the subject. General sources from the Victorian period have also been included, both for their value in identifying other Victorian sources and for their own value as indicators of Victorian thought and standards.

Architecture

Research Guides

151. Kamen, Ruth H. *British and Irish Architectural History: A Bibliography and Guide to Sources of Information.* London: The Architectural Press, 1981.
This guide to British and Irish architectural history covers societies, periodicals, photographs, slides, films, and books but not online and other computer sources. Indexed by author, organizations, subject, and title.

152. Ehresmann, Donald L. *Architecture: A Bibliographic
      Guide to Basic Reference Works, Histories and
      Handbooks.* Littleton, Co.: Libraries Unlimited,
      1984.
This guide covers research on the architectural history.
Annotated entries give an idea of contents and use of
volumes, with useful comments on the reputation of the
work. Author/title index and subject index. No discussion
of the uses of computers in this type of research.

Dictionaries and Encyclopedias

153. Sturgis, Russell. *Dictionary of Architecture and
      Building: Biographical, Historical, and
      Descriptive.* 3 vols. New York: Macmillan,
      1905.
This classic dictionary defines terms, surveys the
architecture of particular places, and gives biographical
essays on architects and builders. Photographs and
illustrations. Still informative.

154. Pevsner, Nikolaus, John Fleming, and Hugh Honour.
      The Dictionary of Architecture. Revised and
      enlarged. Woodstock, N.Y.: The Overlook Press,
      1976.
This dictionary covers all nations and periods of
architecture, with especially useful material on England.
Brief bibliographies follow articles. No indexing, but
plentiful cross references.

155. Curl, James Stevens. *English Architecture: An
      Illustrated Glossary.* Newton Abbot, England.:
      David & Charles, 1977.
This glossary is intended to educate the layman in
architectural terms applying to the buildings of England
and Scotland. Definitions are concise and plentifully
illustrated.

Indexes

156. *Avery Index to Architectural Periodicals.* 2nd ed., rev. and enl. Boston: G. K. Hall, 1973. 15 vols. Supplements, 1975- .
This index has varied in format. Currently, it is available in paper, on microfilm, and online through RLIN (see item 678) and DIALOG (see item 676). The index includes articles, obituaries, and reviews from current architectural periodicals. About 80% of this material comes from sources published outside the United States. The standard index for all architectural studies.

Catalogs

157. *Catalogue of the Library of the Royal Institute of British Architects.* 2 vols. London: The Library, 1937-38.
The catalogue consists of an author list, a classified list, and an alphabetical subject index. It includes books, pamphlets, manuscripts, and typescripts.

158. *Catalogue of Architectural Drawings in the Drawings Collection of the Royal Institute of British Architects.* Farnborough.: Gregg International, 1968- .
This catalog lists drawings collected by the RIBA from its foundation in 1834. Eleven of the volumes are devoted to important individual architects, the rest are arranged alphabetically by name. A one-volume index to this set is also available (*Catalogue of the Drawings Collection of the Royal Institute of British Architects: Cumulative Index.* Brookfield, VT: Gregg International, 1989). The index includes sections for names and for places. Birth and death dates are included in the names index. The locations index lists drawings by country and by town.

159. *The Catalog of the Avery Memorial Architectural Library of Columbia University.* 2nd ed., enlarged. 19 vols. Boston: G. K. Hall, 1968. 1st Supplement, 4 vols. 1972. 2nd. supplement, 4 vols., 1974. 3rd supplement. 4 vols. 1974-77. 4th supplement. 4 vols. 1977-79. 5th supplement. 4 vols. 1979-81.

The catalog covers the collection of what is probably the most important architectural collection in the United States. Arrangement is alphabetical by main entry. The first set covers up to early 1968 and is continued by a number of supplements.

160. Harris, John. *Catalogue of British Drawings for Architecture, Decoration, Sculpture, and Landscape Gardening, 1550-1900, in American Collections.* Upper Saddle River, N.J.: The Gregg Press, 1971.

This catalog lists British architectural drawings in major collections. Arrangement is by artist with subheadings by location. Entries include descriptions of drawings. Many plates illustrate the volume. General index and list of collections analyzed.

Bibliographies

161. Ware, Dora. *A Short Dictionary of British Architects.* London: George Allen and Unwin, 1967.

This dictionary covers British architects of all periods. Entries run one page or less and include basic information on the architect's life and a list of important works.

162. Wodehouse, Lawrence. *British Architects, 1840-1976: A Guide to Information Sources.* Detroit: Gale, 1978.
This book gives brief biographical sketches of British architects along with bibliographies of works on that person. Architects who have not been evaluated by critics are excluded, as are theorists. The index includes the listing "Victorian architecture," facilitating general research in this period.

163. Kaufmann, Edward, and Sharon Irish. *Medievalism: An Annotated Bibliography of Recent Research in the Architecture and Art of Britain and North America.* New York: Garland, 1988.
This volume emphasizes architecture, but book design, sculpture, and the fine arts are also covered. Ruskin and Morris are given special attention as the chief promoters and interpreters of Medievalism. Citations are limited to studies published between 1960 and 1984, though earlier works are noted in annotations.

Guides to Historic Buildings

164. *Historic Houses, Castles, and Gardens, Open to the Public.* East Grinstead, England: British Leisure Publications, 1952- . Title varies.
This annual guide lists by county the historic properties in Great Britain and Ireland. Entries describe notable features, locations, opening times, and available refreshments. Also includes information on viewing Oxford and Cambridge colleges.

Business, Economics, and Labor History

Research Guides

165. Barker, T.C., R.H. Campbell, and P. Mathias. *Business History*. London: The Historical Association, 1960. Revised 1971.
This brief introduction to research in business history offers an overview of the discipline, a list of sources, and information on preparing and writing business history. Emphasis is on British business. Useful "Bibliography of Business History." No index.

Dictionaries and Encyclopedias

166. Eatwell, John, Murray Milgate, and Peter Newman. *The New Palgrave: A Dictionary of Economics.* 4 vols. New York: Stockton Press, 1987.
This four volume "dictionary" might rather be called an encyclopedia of economics. It focuses on the theoretical aspects of economics and includes over 700 biographical entries, including many important Victorian economists and those commenting on economics (Carlyle, Lewis Carroll). Includes cross-references, selected works, and a bibliography.
   The New Palgrave is the successor to an important Victorian reference work: R.H. Palgrave's *Dictionary of Political Economy* (London: Macmillan, 1894). Palgrave's three volume work is an invaluable source for late Victorian economic thought. Like its successor, it focuses on theory, with some attention to biography. Later editions appeared in 1912 and 1925.

Indexes

167. *Index of Economic Articles in Journal and Collective Volumes.* Homewood, Ill.: R.D. Irwin, 1886/1924- . Annual. Title varies: vols. 1-7 called *Index of Economic Journals.* Frequency varies. Contents: Vol. 1, 1886-1924; vol. 2 1925-39; vol. 3 1940-49; vol. 4 1950-54; vol. 5 1954-59; vol. 6, 1960-63; vol. 6A, 1960-63. Collective volumes: vol. 7, 1964-65; vol. 7A 1964-65; vol. 8 1966-67.

Volume one of this index is a valuable source for late Victorian economic articles. Current volumes run behind by about 5 years.

168. *International Bibliography of Economics: Bibliographie de Science Economique.* International Bibliography of the Social Sciences. London: Tavistock, 1955- . Publisher varies.

This annual bibliography in English and French is a list of books, pamphlets, periodical articles, and government publications. Arrangement is by subject classification and includes economic history. Indexed by author and subject.

Bibliographies

169. Stephens, Thomas Arthur. *A Contribution to the Bibliography of the Bank of England.* London: Effingham Wilson, 1897. Rept. 1968.

This bibliography covers the history of the Bank of England from its first charter in 1694 to 1896. Arrangement is chronological. This is a valuable source both as an example of a classic Victorian reference source and as a source for economic history.

170. Batson, Harold E., comp. *A Select Bibliography of Modern Economic Theory, 1870-1929.* London: Routledge & Kegan Paul, 1930.
This book is a classic bibliography of economics. The first section gives select bibliographies on theory. The second part lists the works of various authors. Emphasis is on British and American works. Annotations are concise and give a good indication of content.

171. Bain, G.S., and G.B. Woolven. *A Bibliography of British Industrial Relations.* Cambridge: Cambridge University Press, 1974.
This bibliography lists secondary sources, published in English between 1880 and 1970. Books, pamphlets, articles, theses, and government documents are included. The approach is interdisciplinary, with materials from industrial psychology, industrial sociology, economics, history, law, management, and administration. Arrangement is topical. Personal name and agency or organization index. No annotations.

172. Burnett, John, David Vincent, and David Maynell, eds. *The Autobiography of the Working Class: An Annotated Critical Bibliography.* 2 vols. Brighton: Harvester, 1984. Vol. 1: 1790-1900; Vol. 3: Supplement, 1790-1945.
This set covers autobiographies, diaries, and other autobiographical writings of the nineteenth-century working class. Entries are alphabetical by author and include bibliographical information, family life of the author, occupations, activities, and a summary of the contents of the autobiography, with a comment on the quality of the writing. Appendices list specialized autobiographies, such as diaries and spiritual autobiography. Excellent indexes: General, Places, Occupations, Education, Dates, Authors. Volume 3 supplements earlier volumes with 300 autobiographical works discovered too late to be included. Organized and annotated in the same way as the earlier volumes.

Biography

173. Jeremy, David J., ed. *Dictionary of Business Biography: A Biographical Dictionary of Business Leaders Active in Britain in the Period 1860-1980.* 5 vols. and supplement. London: Butterworths, 1984.

This dictionary gives biographical data for more than 1,000 British entrepreneurs. All aspects of business are covered. Public functions, such as utilities, are included, but the Civil Service is not. Selection emphasizes those who have had a real impact on British business. Articles vary in length from two to seven illustrated pages, including a brief bibliography of both published and unpublished sources. Articles are signed. The supplement includes three indexes (industries, companies and trade associations, people), members of advisory committees, contributors, and a list of errata. An attractive and scholarly volume on important but often neglected figures.

Costume

Dictionaries

174. Cunnington, C. Willett, Phillis Cunnington, and Charles Beard. *A Dictionary of English Costume.* Philadelphia: Dufour Editions, 1960.
This dictionary lists articles of clothing and types of clothing ("aesthetic dress") alphabetically. Line drawings are included for some items. The date when the garment first came into use is noted and a brief description is given.

175. Carman, W.Y. *A Dictionary of Military Uniform.* New York: Scribner's, 1977.
This illustrated dictionary defines the various terms used in describing military clothing. Emphasis is on the British army.

Indexes

176. Monro, Isabel, and Dorothy E. Cook, ed. *Costume Index: A Subject Index to Plates and to Illustrated Texts.* New York: Wilson, 1937. Supplement, ed. by Isabel Stevenson Monro and Kate M. Monro, 1957.
This index lists plates in 615 titles. Any full-page illustration is considered a plate. Indexing is by subject. Nineteenth-century European costume is, with a few exceptions such as folk costume, listed under "Nineteenth Century." Folk costume is entered under the name of the country with appropriate period subdivisions. Useful if your library owns the volumes indexed.

Bibliographies

177. Hiler, Hilaire, and Meyer Hiler, comp. *Bibliography of Costume: A Dictionary Catalog of About Eight Thousand Books and Periodicals.* New York: Wilson, 1939.
This catalog is an author, title, and subject listing of 8400 works on costume. Full bibliographic information is given under author. Emphasis is on English language sources, including books, articles, and catalogs from all periods and countries.

Museums and Collections

178. Huenefeld, Irene Pennington. *International Directory of Historical Clothing.* Metuchen, N.J.: Scarecrow, 1967.
This unique directory lists clothing from the past found in museums, art galleries, historical societies, libraries, and churches in Canada, the United States, and Europe. Its organization is elaborate and allows the researcher to approach the material in several ways. Part I lists North American collections and Part II European. Each section lists holdings by geographic location, by institution, and by category of clothing (accessories, armour, ceremonial clothing), and by category, century, and institutions.

Decorative   Arts   and   Collectibles

179.   Macdonald-Taylor, Margaret, ed. *A Dictionary of*
        Marks: Metalwork,   Furniture,   Ceramics.
        Revised ed. London: The Connoisseur, 1976.
The makers' marks for metalwork, including silver, gold,
and pewter, furniture and tapestry, and ceramics are
listed here. Each category is given its own section and
index.

Antiques

180.   Ramsey, L.G.G. *The Complete Encyclopedia of*
        Antiques. New York: Hawthorn Books, 1962.
This encyclopedia is arranged by type of antique (Carpets
and Rugs, Jewelry) and gives information on terms and
history for each category. Each section includes a glossary
and plates. Lists at the end suggest further reading and
museums and galleries where examples of discussed
antiques may be found. Index.

181.   Miller, Judith, and Martin Miller eds. *The Antiques*
        Directory: Furniture. Boston: G.K. Hall, 1985.
This directory gives pictures and descriptive text for a
variety of antique furnishing. The book is divided first by
country. The British section includes some Scottish and
Irish furniture. Within each country, types of furniture
(beds, bookcases, buckets) are arranged alphabetically.
Review sections give color pictures of some items.
Approximate prices are given in each entry. Sections begin
with introductions giving an overview of the country's
furnishing history. Glossary and Index.

Coins

182. Raymond, Wayte, ed. *Coins of the World: 19th Century Issues.* 2nd ed. New York: Wayte Raymond, Incorporated, 1953.
This catalog is an attempt to present a complete listing of nineteenth-century world coinage, with the omission of gold coinage. A General Introduction gives the few other exceptions to completeness. Grouping is geographic, with Great Britain and Ireland and British Colonies in Europe included under Europe and other British colonies grouped together under their continent. Though prices are of course obsolete, other information, including illustrations of both sides of the coins and range of dates, continues to be valuable.

Decorative Arts

183. Osborne, Harold, ed. *The Oxford Companion to the Decorative Arts.* Oxford: Clarendon Press, 1975.
This guide identifies terms and aspects of the decorative arts. Entries vary from short definitions to longer, thematic essays.

184. Fleming, John, and Hugh Honour. *Dictionary of the Decorative Arts.* New York: Harper & Row, 1977.
This illustrated dictionary includes terms and proper names from the decorative arts. Articles are brief and include short bibliographies where appropriate. Appendices of ceramic marks, hall-marks, and makers' marks on silver and pewter.

Furniture

185. Gloag, John. *A Short Dictionary of Furniture.* London: George Allen and Unwin, 1969.
This dictionary is divided into seven sections: I) "The description of furniture," covering history; 2) "The design of furniture," covering design terms; III) Dictionary of names and terms; IV) Furniture makers in Britain and America; V) Books and periodicals on furniture and design; and VI) Periods, types, materials, and craftsmen from 1100 to 1950. No indexing. Illustrations. Still one of the most comprehensive and authoritative reference sources on furniture.

186. *Pictorial Dictionary of British 19th Century Furniture Design.* Woodbridge, Suffolk: Published for the Antique Collectors Club by the Antique Collectors Club, Ltd., 1977.
This dictionary consists of illustrations of Victorian furniture taken from contemporary sources. It is arranged by furniture type and a caption giving maker and date are provided. The concluding section shows general views of Victorian rooms. No index.

Metal Work

187. Jackson, Charles James, Sir. *English Goldsmiths and Their Marks.* 2nd ed, revised and enlarged. New York: Dover, 1964. Reprint 1921 ed., Macmillan.
This volume is still perhaps the most comprehensive listing of English goldsmith marks. Arrangement is geographical and chronological. Useful historical chapters are interspaced with tables. Indexed by letter in mark.

188. Cotterell, Howard Herschel. *Old Pewter: Its Makers and Marks in England, Scotland and Ireland.* New York: Scribner's; London: Batsford, 1929.
This classic reference covers all aspects of British and Irish pewter. Earlier periods are emphasized, but a good amount of Victorian craft is covered. Ten chapters give historical information, information on touch plates and secondary marks, illustrations of pewter-ware, alphabetical list of pewterers with their marks, alphabetical list of marks, list of "obscure" marks, and indexes to various chapters on marks. Includes bibliography and general index.

189. Chaffers, William. *Hall Marks on Gold and Silver Plate of Great Britain and Ireland.* Text and date table extended, corrected and revised by Cyril G.E. Bunt. 10th ed revised. London: William Reeves, 1969.
This book is useful to those approaching hallmarks for the first time. Not only does it list specific marks, it includes a chapter on "How to Read 'Hall Mark,'" and gives a history of the use of marks in various countries.

Needlework

190. Clabburn, Pamela. *The Needleworker's Dictionary.* New York: William Morrow, 1976.
This dictionary gives brief identifications of people, terms, and works of needlework. Emphasis is European but other areas are covered. Plentifully illustrated.

Pottery and Porcelain

191. Solon, M.L. *Ceramic Literature: An Analytical Index to the Works Published in All Languages on the History and the Technology of the Ceramic Art.* London: Charles Griffin, 1910.
This index lists all types of printed material in all languages on the subject of ceramics. Coverage is best for Western European languages. Many of the entries are for Victorian sources. Arrangement is alphabetical by author, with a topically arranged short title index.

192. Godden, Geoffrey A. *Encyclopaedia of British Pottery and Porcelain Marks.* New York: Crown, 1964.
This encyclopedia contains over 4000 British china marks from 1650 to the 1960s. The main section of the book is a list of marks arranged alphabetically by manufacturer's name. Marks are identified by means of initials, names, or devices appearing on the pottery. Plentiful cross references help in this task, and a list of complicated monograms or signs is included. It includes a glossary, bibliography, and indexes of monograms and of signs and devices. The definitive source on pottery and porcelain marks.

193. Mankowitz, Wolf, and Reginald G. Haggar. *The Concise Encyclopedia of English Pottery and Porcelain.* New York: Praeger, 1968.
This encyclopedia lists terms, initials, people, places, and companies connected to the English pottery and porcelain industry. Chapters cover: "Names of Potters, Pottery Firms, Pot-Dealers and Outside Decorators," "Engravers for Pottery & Porcelain," "Books and Articles Giving Lists of Names of Potters and Pottery Craftsmen," "British and American Museums Where Pottery and Porcelain May Be Studied," "British Potters on Foreign Soil, and "Classified Bibliography." Several indexes.

194. Campbell, James Edward. *Pottery and Ceramics: A Guide to Information Sources.* Detroit: Gale, 1978.

This book lists books, periodicals, and collections on pottery and ceramics. English pottery and porcelain receive their own section. Bibliographic entries are descriptively annotated. Author, title, and subject indexes.

195. Cameron, Elizabeth. *Encyclopedia of Pottery and Porcelain, 1800-1960.* New York: Facts on File, 1986.

This encyclopedia covers pottery and porcelain of the nineteenth and twentieth centuries from all over the world. Arrangement is alphabetical and entries cover people, companies, and terms. Illustrations.

History of Education

Research Guides

196.   Foskett, D.J. *How to Find Out: Educational Research.*
       Oxford: Pergamon Press, 1965.
This guide to research includes a section on information
sources in the history of education. Outdated for specific
sources, it still is useful for background and pioneering
studies.

Dictionaries and Encyclopedias

197.   Fletcher, Alfred Ewen, ed. *Sonnenschein's*
       Encyclopaedia of Education. London: Swan
       Sonnenschein, 1889.
This one-volume encyclopedia covers in alphabetical order
a variety of educational terms and concepts. Brief
biographical articles are included. The valuable source for
late Victorian educational theory includes "A Select and
Systematic Bibliography of Pedagogy" by William Swan
Sonnenschein.

198. Mitzel, Harold E., ed. *The Encyclopedia of Educational*
     Research. 4 vols. 5th ed. New York: The Free
     Press; London: Collier Macmillan, 1982.
Editions of this encyclopedia go back to 1941, and it is a
major   source   for   summary   and   interpretation   of
educational research. Emphasis is on current developments
in education, but historical materials are included. It also
includes short articles on major Victorian educational
theorists.

Indexes

199. The Librarians of Institutes of Education, comps. *British Education Index.* London: The Library Association, 1961- . Quarterly with annual cumulations. Frequency of larger cumulations vary.
These volumes index British periodicals in the area of education, including history of education. Arrangement is by subject, with an author index. Part of this index is also available in microfiche as *British Education Theses Index,* and the entire index is available as DIALOG file 121, from 1950 to the present. The file is also included in the ERIC database available through DIALOG.

Biographical Sources

200. Roscoe, J.E. *The Dictionary of Educationists.* 5th ed. London: Rea & Inchbould, 1915.
This dictionary gives biographical sketches, from one paragraph to several pages in length, on leading figures in education from the Middle Ages to the early twentieth century. Emphasis is on British educators, many from the nineteenth century.

201. Christopher, Ann. *An Index to Nineteenth Century British Educational Biography.* London: Institute of Education, University of London, 1965. Published as the 10th supplement to *Education Libraries Bulletin.*
This listing of biographies of nineteenth century educators is limited to English-language sources found in books. Theological education is excluded. Those active between 1800 and 1900 are covered. Arrangement is alphabetical by subject of biography. Topical subject index.

History

Research Guides

202. Hepworth, Philip. *How to Find Out in History.* Oxford: Pergamon, 1966.
Despite the age of this guide, it is valuable for its British emphasis and its attention to local history in Britain. Use as a supplement to the methodological concerns of the two guides listed below.

203. Kitson Clark, G. *Guide for Research Students Working on Historical Subjects.* 2nd ed. Cambridge: Cambridge University Press, 1968.
This little guide covers basic research methodology. Emphasis is on acquiring and evaluating evidence, with only a brief appendix on specific titles. A classic description of the historian's art.

204. Frick, Elizabeth. *Library Research Guide to History: Illustrated Search Strategy and Sources.* Ann Arbor: Pierian Press, 1980.
The strength of this guide lies in its clear, concise explanation of the research process as applied to history. Aimed at the beginning, undergraduate researcher, it goes beyond merely listing sources, teaching students to find and evaluate new sources.

Dictionaries and Encyclopedias

205. Wiener, Philip P., ed. *Dictionary of the History of Ideas: Studies of Selected Pivotal Ideas.* 5 vols. New York: Charles Scribner's Sons, 1973.
This encyclopedia is a series of lengthy essays in intellectual history. Emphasis is on the interactions of various subject fields in the development of ideas. Essays cover the history of an idea ("Ambiguity as aesthetic principle," "Nationalism"), the problems presented by the concept, and a bibliography of further readings. Articles are signed. A unique and too often overlooked source.

General Bibliographies

206. Gilmore, William J. *Psychohistorical Inquiry: A Comprehensive Bibliography.* New York: Garland, 1984.
This bibliography covers "general studies about a civilization, studies of the contemporary life cycle and its stages, and studies of individuals" written from a psychohistorical perspective. The majority of articles are in English, with a representative sample of other languages. Part I covers essays and books on methodology. Part II covers studies divided by geographic area, and, in some cases, time period. Lengthy introduction, no annotations, author index.

207. Henige, David, comp. *Serial Bibliographies and Abstracts in History: An Annotated Guide.* Westport, Conn.: Greenwood, 1986.
This guide lists bibliographies appearing in or as serials in the field of history. "History" is broadly defined, covering scientific, cultural, and intellectual history as well as socio-political subjects. Arrangement is alphabetical by source and annotations indicate frequency, scope, and currency. Subject index.

Indexes and Annual Bibliographies

208. *Annual Bibliography of Historical Literature.*
     London: The Historical Association, 1912- .
     Annual

This annual publication contains critical bibliographic essays on historical writings for a particular year. All areas of world history are covered, but emphasis is clearly British. The section on the nineteenth century covers 1815-1914 economic, social, political, religious, scientific, medical, and intellectual history. Ireland is treated in a separate division.

209. *Population Index.* Princeton, N.J.: Office of
     Population Research, Princeton University, and
     the Population Association of America, 1935- .
     Quarterly.

This annotated bibliography includes books and periodical literature on all aspects of population, including historical studies. Arrangement is by class, with annual cumulated indexes by author and by country. Entries from 1938 to 1968 have been cumulated as *Population Index Bibliography* (Boston: G.K. Hall, 1971, 9 vols.).

210. *Historical Abstracts, 1777-1945: Bibliography of the World's Periodical Literature.* vols. 1-16. Santa Barbara: Clio Press, with the International Social Science Institute, 1955-1970. Quarterly. Five Year Index: vols. 1-5, 1963; vols. 6-10, 1965; v. 11-15, 1970; v. 16-20, 1979. Vol. 17- . Santa Barbara: American Bibliographic Center, 1971-. Quarterly. Retrospective Index, vols. 26-30: Santa Barbara: American Bibliographic Center, 1980-.

This abstract covers historical periodicals, mostly from the United States. After 1964, United States and Canadian history are listed in a separate abstract, *America: History and Life.* Victorian history is covered in Part A: *Modern History Abstracts*, Section 5. The index is searchable online back to 1973 in DIALOG file 39.

British and Irish History

Chronologies

211. Cheney, C.R. *Handbook for Students of English History.* London: Offices of the Royal Historical Society, 1945.

This handbook gives tables of various dates in English history. Sections include: Reckonings of Time, Rulers of England, Lists of Popes from Gregory I to Pius XII, Saints' Days and Festivals Used in Dating, Legal Chronology, the Roman Calendar, Calendars for All Possible Dates of Easter, English Calendar for A.D 1752, Chronological Table of Easter Days A.D. 500-2000, and Index.

212.   Powicke, Frederick M., and Edmond B. Fryde.
       Handbook of British Chronology. 2nd ed. London:
       Offices of the Royal Historical Society, 1961.
This book lists British office holders and nobility,
parliaments and related assemblies, and provincial and
national councils of the Church of England. Beginning and
end dates vary with list.

Dictionaries and Encyclopedias

213.   Steinberg, S.H., and I.H. Evans, eds. *Steinberg's
       Dictionary of British History.* 2nd ed. New
       York: St. Martin's Press, 1971.
This dictionary covers the history of Britain and its
overseas possessions as long as their connection with
Britain lasted. Political, constitutional, administrative,
legal, ecclesiastical, and economic history are covered in a
dictionary form. Articles are initialed by contributors.

214.   Donaldson, Gordon, and Robert S. Morpeth. *A
       Dictionary of Scottish History.* Edinburgh: John
       Donald Publishers Ltd., 1977.
This dictionary identifies with brief entries people,
places, and events from all periods of Scottish history.

215.   Hickey, D.J., and J.E. Doherty. *A Dictionary of Irish
       History Since 1800.* Totowa, N.J.: Barnes &
       Noble, 1980.
This dictionary covers political, social, religious,
economic, and other types of history. Entries are under
both topics and personal names. Useful short articles and
good cross references.

216.   Kenyon, J.P., ed. *A Dictionary of British History.*
New York: Stein and Day, 1983.
"This book covers the history of the British Isles and its
overseas possessions from the Roman conquest until
1970." A dictionary section covers political, social,
scientific, and cultural history, followed by a chronology,
and a family tree of the royal houses starting with Wessex.

217.   Haigh, Christopher, ed. *The Cambridge Encyclopedia
of Great Britain and Ireland.* Cambridge:
Cambridge University Press, 1985.
Chapter 6 of this encyclopedia of British history deals with
"Political Reform and Economic Revolution, 1783-1901."
Within the chapter are an overview of the period and
signed articles on Government and Politics, 1983-1846;
Government and Politics, 1846-1901; Ireland; Warfare
and International Relations; The British Economy; Society;
and Culture. The margins contain a list of important terms
with definitions. The book ends with a who's who, a list of
further reading and an index.

Indexes and Annual Bibliographies

218.   *Annual Bibliography of British and Irish History.*
Brighton, Sussex: Harvester Press; New York:
St. Martin's Press, for the Royal Historical
Society, 1975- .
This annual bibliography covers journals and books on
Britsh and Irish history. Victorian material is under
"Britain 1815-1914" and "Ireland since c. 1640."
Subheadings and subject and author indexes contribute to
ease of access.

Bibliographies

219. Terry, C.S. *Catalogue of the Publications of Scottish Historical and Kindred Clubs and Societies, and of the Volumes Relative to Scottish History Issued by His Majesty's Stationary Office, 1780-1908.* 2 vols. Glasgow: Maclehose, 1909.
This catalog covers the publications of 27 clubs and societies in existence in 1909. Arrangement is by society name. Bibliographic information and a list of the articles included are given for the pamphlets. Identifies much fugitive material.

220. Williams, Judith Blow. *A Guide to the Printed Materials for English Social and Economic History, 1750-1850.* 2 vols. New York: Columbia University Press, 1926.
This two volume set covers its subject thoroughly and can be used as a finding aid for many Victorian studies. Brief, helpful annotations.

221. Jenkins, R.T., and William Rees, eds. *A Bibliography of the History of Wales.* Cardiff: University of Wales Press Board, 1931.
This bibliography covers all periods of Welsh history through the nineteenth century. The section on the nineteenth century includes materials on political history, social and economic history, the history of education, and religion. A separate section covers materials on local history. Excellent for nineteenth-century sources on Wales.

222. *Writings on British History.* Vol. 5, 1815-1914. 2 parts. London: Jonathan Cape, 1970.

This bibliography lists writings from 1901 to 1933 on the subject of British history. "History" is broadly defined, with sections on economic, social, ecclesiastical, cultural, scientific, military, and local history. Biography is also covered. Annual supplements update the bibliography to 1974.

223. Brown, Lucy M., and Ian R. Christie. *Bibliography of British History, 1789-1851.* Oxford: Clarendon, 1977.

This selective bibliography covers primary, secondary, and bibliographic sources for early nineteenth-century British history. Arrangement is by type of history, with appropriate subdivisions. Some brief annotations. Indexed by author and subject. Late Victorian history is covered in H.J. Hanham's *Bibliography of British History, 1851-1914* (Oxford: Clarendon, 1976).

224. Cohen, Ben. *The Thames, 1580-1980: A General Bibliography.* London: Ben Cohen F.R.C.S., 1985.

This bibliography includes many valuable and often obscure sources on the Thames. However, it is difficult to use for historical research. Its organization is topical, with 19 classified sections including such subjects as Barrage, Barriers, Floods, Drainage; Embankments; Exhibitions, Art Publications, Views. The ninth section, "General, Historic, Literary," covers some of the historical material, but other sections also contain historic accounts. Arrangement within the sections is alphabetic. No indexing. With better access points, this could be a valuable research tool for a little-explored subject.

Agricultural History

225. Stratton, John M., and Jack H. Brown. *Agricultural Records in Britain, AD 200-1977.* Hamden, CT: Archon Books, 1979.

This book is based upon Thomas H. Baker's 1912 *Records of the Seasons, Prices of Agricultural Produce, and Phenomena Observed in the British Isles.* It gives a year-by-year report on the weather, crop yields, agricultural prices, and any other matter important to farming and farmers. This collection of information is unique and an important foundation for agricultural history, with possible applications to other fields.

History of the Empire

226. Lewin, Evans. *Best Books on the British Empire: A Bibliographical Guide for Students.* Royal Empire Society Bibliographies, No. 12. 2nd ed. London: The Royal Empire Society, 1945.

The majority of the books in this selective bibliography were published between 1910 and 1944. It is still an excellent source for studies of the Empire.

227. Flint, John E. *Books on the British Empire and Commonwealth: A Guide for Students.* London: Published on behalf of The Royal Commonwealth Society by Oxford University Press, 1968.

This list of "best" books on the Empire and the Commonwealth supplements the contents of the previous item. Emphasis is on historical and political literature. Books listed are mostly those published since 1940.

228. Heussler, Robert. *British Malaya: A Bibliographical and Biographical Compendium.* Themes in European Expansion. New York: Garland, 1981.
Many of the entries in this bibliography concern nineteenth-century colonial rule. Descriptive annotations, subject and author indexes. The series, of which this is the first volume, is a useful source of titles on the Empire. See also entries 229 through 232.

229. Bailey, Susan F. *Women and the British Empire: An Annotated Guide to Sources.* Themes in European Expansion. New York: Garland, 1983.
This guide explores sources on the role of women in the establishment of the rule of the British Empire. Four chapters cover "Wives of Administrators," "Settlers," "Missionaries," and "Native Women." Each section has a bibliographic essay evaluating the sources. A Bibliography with brief annotations follows. Indexed by author, title, and subject.

230. Musiker, Naomi, with Reuben Musiker. *South African History: A Bibliographical Guide with Special Reference to Territorial Expansion and Colonization.* Themes in European Expansion. New York: Garland, 1984.
This bibliography is a topical listing of materials on European contact with South Africa. It begins with seventeenth century exploration and travel and continues to 1980. The bulk of the entries deal with nineteenth century colonialism. Entries are annotated. Author/Title index and Subject/Topographical index.

231. Ofcansky, Thomas P. *British East Africa, 1856-1963.* Themes in European Expansion. New York: Garland, 1985.

Though the coverage of this bibliography goes beyond the Victorian period, it will be of interest to the Victorianist for its coverage of exploration and colonialism in this region. Author index.

232. Palmegiano, Eugenia M. *The British Empire in the Victorian Press, 1832-1867.* New York: Garland, 1987.

This bibliography lists nearly 300 entries from about 50 London-based magazines. These entries represent press coverage of all aspects of the British Empire between the Reform Acts. Arrangement is by magazine, with an author and a subject index. Subjects are broad and general.

233. Bayly, C.A., ed. *Atlas of the British Empire.* New York; Oxford: Facts on File, 1989.

This atlas covers the British Empire from exploration beginning in 1500 to the ongoing decline of the Empire. The text is at an introductory level, with boxes giving brief accounts of various special subjects. The second and third sections, "The Age of Free Enterprise: 1763-1860" and "The Heyday of Empire: 1860-1914," cover various aspects of the Empire during the Victorian period. The 39 maps do not offer any new or novel information about the Empire, but may be useful for their graphic presentation of frequently used statistics and geographical facts.

Foreign Relations

234. Weigall, David, with the editorial assistance of Christopher Catherwood. *Britain and the World 1815-1986: A Dictionary of International Relations.* New York: Oxford University Press, 1987.
This book covers British foreign policy and international relations in dictionary form. "It includes historical and biographical entries and definitions of the terms and concepts used in diplomacy and international relations." Brief bibliographies follow many of the entries. Includes a chronological table and maps.

Local and Municipal History

Research Guides

235. Emmison, F.G. *Archives and Local History.* 2nd ed. Chichester, Eng.: Phillimore & Co., 1974.
This guide is primarily aimed at the beginning researcher. It covers various aids available, the types of local repositories, preparing to visit repositories, the use of local archives, and a list of selected pamphlets and articles. Indexed.

236. Stephens, W.B. *Sources for English Local History.* Cambridge: Cambridge University Press, 1981.
"This book is intended to provide an introduction to the detailed study of the general history of a region, town, village, or other local area, or of particular aspects of local history." Information is presented in the form of bibliographic essays with footnotes providing exact bibliographic information. Index.

237. Riden, Philip. *Local History: A Handbook for Beginners.* London: Batsford Academic and Educational Ltd., 1983.
This book is an introduction to the study of local history in Great Britain. The first chapter describes the field of local history and traces its development. The next five chapters cover research on various sources: the library, the records office, maps, landscapes and buildings, and the public records office. The final chapter deals with preparation and publication of articles. Includes list of useful addresses, further reading, and index.

238. Riden, Philip. *Record Sources for Local History.* London: B.T. Batsford Ltd., 1987.
This volume covers sources for local history found in both central and local records offices. Arrangement is chronological, with separate subsections in each chapter on the various subject of research. Chapters are in the form of essays. Appendixes include: 1) Classes of the Public Records referred to in the text; 2) The Division of Records at the PRO; 3) Water Records. Includes Bibliography and Index.

Directories

239. Goss, Charles W.F. *The London Directories, 1677-1855.* London: Denis Archer, 1932.
This catalog lists in chronological order directories of London appearing 1677 to 1855. A lengthy introduction discusses the history of directories and describes the information included in the volumes listed in this catalog. No index.

240. Shaw, Gareth, and Allison Tipper. *British Directories: A Bibliography to Directories Published in England, Wales, (1850-1950), and Scotland (1773-1950).* London: Leicester University Press, 1989.
This directory extends the guides of Goss (item 239) and Jane Norton, (*Guide to the National and Provincial Directories of England and Wales, Excluding London, Published Before 1856.* London: Offices of the Royal Historical Society, 1950). It adds coverage for Scotland and extends it for England, including London, and Wales, past 1856 to 1950. Scottish directories to 1950 are also covered. In addition, it includes trade directories not covered in Goss or Norton. Three sections cover an introduction to British directories, a bibliography of directories, and a guide to libraries holding large collections of directories.

Bibliographies

241. Martin, G.H., and Sylvia McIntyre. *A Bibliography of British and Irish Municipal History.* Leicester: Leicester University Press, 1972.
This title continues Charles Gross's *A Bibliography of British Municipal History, Including Guilds and Parliamentary Representation.* (New York: Longmans Green, 1897). Both bibliographies cover books, pamphlets, articles, and papers on British municipal history. Martin follows Gross's organization, with Part I containing general works and Part II covering specific towns. Indexing by personal and proper names. Martin covers "from earliest time to the end of 1966," but excludes all materials in Gross.

Indexes

242. Pugh, R.B., ed. *The Victoria History of the Counties of England: General Introduction.* Oxford: Published for The Institute of Historical Research by Oxford University Press, 1970.

This volume is an essential introduction and finding aid for the *Victoria History of the Counties of England.* It gives the history of the project, a list of volumes and their contents, an index by article title, and an index of authors.

Military and Naval History

Research Guides

243. Higham, Robin, ed. *A Guide to the Sources of British Military History.* Berkeley: University of California Press, 1971.

This volume is a comprehensive bibliography on British military history from prehistoric times to 1970. The nineteenth century is well covered, with chapters on "The Army in the Nineteenth Century," "The Navy in the Nineteenth Century," "Economic, Scientific, and Technological Background for Military Studies, 1815-1914," and "Colonial Warfare, 1815-1970." Separate chapters cover "The Evolution of Military Medicine," "The Evolution of Naval Medicine," and "The History of Military and Martial Law." Each section is written by a specialist and signed. The bibliography has been supplemented by Gerald Jordan's *British Military History: A Supplement to Robin Higham's "Guide to the Sources."* (New York: Garland, 1988).

Regimental History

244. Chister, H.M., and G. Burges-Short. *The Records and Badges of Every Regiment and Corps in the British Army.* 2nd ed. London: Gale and Polden, 1900. Rept. 1970. Frederick Muller.
This book is described by the title. Color illustrations show badges, flags, and uniforms of the British army at the time of writing. The text gives the history of the various regiments and corps. First edition, 1895.

245. Farmer, John S. *The Regimental Records of the British Army: A Historical Resume Chronologically Arranged, of Titles, Campaigns, Honours, Uniforms, Facings, Badges, Nicknames, Etc.* Bristol: Crecy Books, 1901. Rept. 1984.
This volume lists the regiments of the British Army. Arrangement is by branch of service. Entries give the name of the regiment, its seal and crest, titles, principal campaigns and battles, description of uniforms at various dates, badges, nicknames, historical note, and bibliographic references. It includes a bibliography of regimental histories. Illustrated.

Land Forces

246. Frederick, J.B.M., comp. *Lineage Book of British Land Forces, 1660-1978: Biographical Outlines of Cavalry, Yeomanry, Armour, Artillery, Infantry, Marines and Air Force land Troops of the Regulars and Reserve Forces.* 2 vols. Wakefield, Yorkshire: Microform Academic Publishers, 1984.
This guide to the history of British land forces is organized by type of force and dates. The guide is filled with useful and detailed information but little guidance to use. Expertise on the subject is assumed.

Naval History

247. Gossett, W.P. *The Lost Ships of the Royal Navy,*
      1793-1900. London: Mansell, 1986.
This guide lists ships lost by the Royal Navy through
enemy action, mutiny, shipwrecks, or fire. Three points of
access are given: by date, name, and place of loss.

248. Colledge, J.J. *Ships of the Royal Navy: An Historical*
      Index. 2 vols. New York: Augustus M. Kelley,
      Publishers, 1969.
These volumes list alphabetically British warships from
the fifthteenth to the twentieth century. Short annotations
give the ship's characteristics and fate. Includes tonnage,
dimensions, armament, materials, and building yard.

History of Parliament

249. Wilding, Norman, and Philip Laundy. *A n*
      Encyclopedia of Parliament. Completely revised
      4th ed. London: Cassell, 1972.
This encyclopedia explains the concepts of parliamentary
government. Of interest to the Victorianist is the article
"Victoria (1819-1901) and Parliament."

250. Goehlert, Robert U., and Fenton S. Martin. *The*
      Parliament of Great Britain: A Bibliography.
      Lexington, Mass.: D.C. Heath, 1983.
This books attempts to be a comprehensive bibliography of
materials in English on Parliament. It is divided into ten
areas: 1) Origins and Development; 2) Legislative
Process; 3) House of Commons; 4) House of Lords; 5)
Organization; 6) Pressures on Parliament; 7) Reform of
Parliament; 8) Parliament and the Electorate; 9)
Members of Parliament; and 10) Support and Housing of
Parliament. Not annotated. Indexed by author and by
subject.

Transportation History

251. Hocking, Charles. *Dictionary of Disasters at Sea During the Age of Steam: Including Sailing Ships and Ships of War Lost in Action, 1842-1962.* 2 vols. Crawley, England.: Lloyd's Register of Shipping, 1969.
These volumes list in alphabetical order ships of all nationalities that met with disasters at sea. Entries include physical description of ship and short account of disaster.

252. Kemp, Peter, ed. *The Oxford Companion to Ships & the Sea.* London: Oxford University Press, 1976.
This volume follows the usual pattern for the Oxford Companions. It offers short definitions and identifications of terms, people, and historical events associated with ships and sailing. Emphasis is British.

253. Ottley, George, comp. *A Bibliography of British Railway History.* 2nd ed. London: HMSO, 1983.
This bibliography covers books, parts of books, pamphlets, and journals on the subject of the history of the railway in Britain. Arrangement is by subject and then chronological. Some annotations. Excellent index by author, title, and subject.

Women's History

254. Kanner, Barbara, ed. *Women of England: From Anglo-Saxon Times to the Present: Interpretive Bibliographical Essays.* Hamden, Conn.: Archon Books, 1979.
This anthology consists of twelve bibliographic essays, with Barbara Kanner's introductory essay covering the full span of English women's history. Sheila Ryan Johansson's "Demographic Contributions to the History of Victorian Women" and Patricia Otto Klaus's "Women in the Mirror: Using Novels to Study Victorian Women" offer more specific guidance for Victorian studies.

255. Kanner, Barbara. *Women in English Social History, 1800-1914: An Essay and Guide to Research in Thirteen Categories of Inquiry.* 3 vols. New York: Garland, 1987-1990.
These three volumes cover women in nineteenth century English social history. Categories include: "The Expansion of Employment, " "Philanthropy, Social Service, and Social Reform," "Crime and Deviance," "Sexual Issues," "Science, Social Sciences, and Their Social Application," "Women's Rights, Feminism, Politics and Suffrage." Entries give title, author, date, and, in some cases, a content note. Each volume is separately indexed.

Periodicals

256. Harrison, Royden, Gillian B. Woolven, and Robert Duncan, comps. *The Warwick Guide to British Labour Periodicals, 1790-1970: A Check List.* Hassocks, England: Harvester, 1977.
This checklist is arranged alphabetically by main entry. The entries contain title, starting and finishing dates, numbers and volumes, frequency, and a category. Some entries contain brief information about publisher or content. Indexes by date and by subject.

257. Steiner, Dale R. *Historical Journals: A Handbook for Writers and Reviewers.* Santa Barbara, Ca.: ABC-Clio, 1981.
The major part of this book is an alphabetical listing of historical journals, with descriptions of scope, requirements for manuscripts, policy on reviews, and address. Introductory material gives information on publishing in these journals.

258. Boehm, Eric H., Barbara H. Pope, and Marie S. Ensign, eds. *Historical Periodicals Directory.* Santa Barbara, Ca.: ABC-Clio, 1983.
This guide to historical periodicals and selected series is issued in five volumes. Entries are arranged alphabetically by title within sections by country of publication. Entries include information on publisher, agent, address, subjects covered, language, cumulative indexes available, inclusion in indexing or abstracting services, and former titles. The fifth volume includes a cumulative subject index and a title index.

Dissertations

259. Kuehl, Warren F. *Dissertations in History: An Index to Dissertations Compiled in History Departments of United States and Canadian Universities, 1873-1960.* Lexington: University of Kentucky Press, 1965; Supplement, 1961-1970, 1972.
Dissertations in History, 1970-June 1980: An Index to Dissertations Completed in History Departments of United States and Canadian Universities. Santa Barbara, Ca.: ABC-Clio Information Service, 1985.
These indexes list dissertations written for departments of history in the United States and Canada. Arrangement is alphabetical by author. Detailed subject indexes.

260. Bell, S. Peter. *Dissertations on British History, 1815-1914: An Index to British and American Theses.* Metuchen, N.J.: Scarecrow, 1974.
This list of about 2,300 British and American dissertations covers the history of Great Britain and Ireland between 1815 and 1914, plus wider periods and topics containing significant material on this period. British and Irish dissertations for both the masters and doctors degree are included; American and Canadian dissertations for the doctoral degree only. The five section are: Political History, Economic History, Social History, Ecclesiastical History, and History of Education. Indexes by author, persons, places, and subject.

261. *Doctoral Dissertations in History.* Washington, D.C.: American Historical Association Institutional Services Program, 1976- .
This listing continues *List of Doctoral Dissertations in History in Progress or Recently Completed in the United States* (1906-1976). Entries are arranged by broad topics, nationally for the modern period. Entries include author's name, dissertation title, academic affiliation, brief description of the work, and availability of the work.

Library Catalogs

262. *Subject Catalogue of the Library of The Royal Empire Society.* 4 vols. 1930-37. Rept, with new intro., 1967.
Subject Catalogue of The Royal Commonwealth Society, London. 7 vols., 2 supplements. Boston: G.K. Hall, 1971.
These two sets, along with the *Biography Catalogue,* list the holdings of the library of the society founded in 1868 as The Colonial Society. The collection deals with all aspects of the Empire and, later, the Commonwealth and their members past and present. Holdings listed go up to March 1971. Arrangement is geographical.

Biography

263. Walson, Charles A. *The Writing of History in Britain: A Bibliography of Post-1945 Writings About British Historians and Biographers.* New York: Garland, 1982.
This bibliography of writings on historians and biographers is organized by century. Books, articles, and dissertations published in English after 1945 are included. Short, descriptive annotations. Author and subject index.

Literature and Language

Research Guides

264. Sanders, Chauncey. *An Introduction to Research in English Literary History.* New York: Macmillan, 1952.

This is a classic guide to research and is still useful for its introduction to methodology. The title does not do justice to the breadth of coverage here. Among its many topics, it deals with editing, biography, attribution, source study, chronology, and influence.

265. Thorpe, James E. *The Use of Manuscripts in Literary Research: Problems of Access and Literary Property Rights.* 2nd ed. New York: Modern Language Association of America, 1979.

This guide tells how to effectively use manuscripts in literary research. It covers such topics as locating manuscripts, gaining access to private collections, permission to publish, and literary property rights. An invaluable aid to those beginning manuscript research.

266. Altick, Richard D. *The Art of Literary Research.* Revised by John J. Fenstermaker. 3rd. ed. New York: Norton, 1981.

This delightful guide to literary research is as enjoyable as it is useful to the beginning scholar. It is a guide first to scholarly modes of thought and techniques of research. Specific titles of use to the researcher are listed in "For Further Reading," and the strengths and charms of major libraries in the U.S. and U.K. are discussed.

267. Baker, Nancy L. *A Research Guide for Undergraduate Students: English and American Literature.* 2nd ed. New York: The Modern Language Association of America, 1985.

This guide introduces students to research techniques and sources for the study of English-language literature. Good traditional approach but does not take into account newer, electronic and microform sources of information.

268. Miller, R.H. *Handbook of Literary Research.* Metuchen, N.J.: Scarecrow, 1987.

This handbook introduces students to the major research sources for English and American literature. The first chapter is an introduction to general reference books, the second chapter lists guides to scholarship on topics in literature, and chapter three through seven deal in depth with research problems common to both American and English literature, such as locating works about a subject or about an author. These chapters include a flow chart indicating the most efficient research path and an annotated list of the books in the flow chart. Chapters eight and nine deal with finding manuscripts and dissertations. Indexed by author and title.

269. Harner, James L. *Literary Research Guide: A Guide to Reference Sources for the Study of Literatures in English and Related Topics.* New York: Modern Language Association of America, 1989.

This guide is an invaluable tool for those, from advanced undergraduates to experienced scholars, doing research in literary fields. The Introduction is a discussion of research techniques and the use of the guide. The body of the work is a topically arranged list of reference works on literature and related fields. Annotations are critical, evaluative, and a model of what an annotation should be.

Dictionaries and Encyclopedias

270. Chambers, Robert. *Chamber's Cyclopaedia of English Literature.* 4th ed., revised by Robert Carruthers. London: W. & R. Chambers, 1883.
This two volume set gives biographical and critical evaluations of English literary figures and movements. The various editions chart the ebb and flow of literary reputations during the period.

271. Barnhart, Clarence L., with the assistance of William D. Halsey, eds. *New Century Handbook of English Literature.* Revised ed. New York: Appleton/Century/Crofts, 1967.
This handbook identifies names and terms from English and Irish literature. It provides in one place information that is spread over many other sources. Included are entries for authors, titles of literary works, fictional characters, technical terms, nicknames and sobriquets, and places.

272. Freeman, William. *Dictionary of Fictional Characters.* Revised by Fred Urquhart, with Indexes of authors and titles by E.N. Pennell. Boston: The Writer, Inc., 1974.
This dictionary lists 20,000 fictitious characters from about 200 British, Commonwealth, and American books. Brief identification of characters, with an emphasis on nineteenth century fiction and poetry.

273. Preminger, Alex, ed. *Princeton Encyclopedia of Poetry and Poetics.* Princeton: Princeton University Press, 1974.
This encyclopedia is the premier source for information on all aspects of poetry and poetics. Articles range from short definitions to lengthy discussions of national literatures, techniques, and prosody. The *Princeton Handbook of Poetic Terms* (Alex Preminger, ed. Princeton, N.J.: Princeton University Press, 1986) includes definitions from the *Encyclopedia,* and a few new entries, for a concise version.

274. Stapleton, Michael. *The Cambridge Guide to English Literature.* Cambridge: Cambridge University Press, 1983.
This guide to English-language literature gives brief entries on people, works, and characters of the literatures of Great Britain, Ireland, the United States, Australia, Canada, the West Indies, English-speaking Africa, and New Zealand. Entries are short and basic. Useful for identifications and lists of an author's principal works.

275. Drabble, Margaret, and Jenny Stringer, eds. *The Oxford Companion to English Literature.* 5th ed. Oxford: Oxford University Press, 1985.
This book provides short identifications of the writers, characters and works of British literature. "English literature" is given an extremely wide definition, including not only Irish and other national literatures · from the British Isles, but also important foreign and classical authors who have influenced British writers. Non-literary figures and events are also included when culturally important

276. *Benet's Reader's Encyclopedia.* 3rd ed. New York: Harper & Row, 1987.
This encyclopedia gives brief sketches on people, titles, movements, and terms of world literature, with useful overview essays on national literatures.

277. Sutherland, John. *The Stanford Guide to Victorian Fiction.* Palo Alto: Stanford University Press, 1989.
This guide lists information on Victorian novels and novelists, including 878 biographical entries, 554 synopses of novels, 47 entries on Victorian magazines, 63 entries on publishers, 38 entries on literary schools and terms describing types of literature, and 26 entries on illustrators. The appendices cover proper names and pseudonyms and maiden and married names.

Chronologies

278.   Rogal, Samuel J. *A Chronological Outline of British Literature.* Westport, Conn.: Greenwood Press, 1980.
This chronology is intended to give the social context of British literature. Four categories are listed by year: Births, Deaths, Events, and Works. Indexed by personal name, anonymous titles, and periodical titles.

279.   Smallwood, P.J. *A Concise Chronology of English Literature.* Totowa, N.J.: Barnes & Noble Books, 1985.
This chronology is organized first by century, then by year. The verso lists literary events; the recto non-literary events. Index by authors' names.

Atlases and Gazetteers

280.   Hardwick, Michael. *A Literary Atlas & Gazetteer of the British Isles.* Cartography by Alan G. Hodgkiss. Detroit: Gale Research, 1973.
Over 4500 entries list places with literary associations. Maps are by county, with a numerical list of sites, and cover England, Scotland, and Wales. Indexes by person, one alphabetical, one by county. Sites are all associated with authors' lives; no locations for fictional events.

281.   Eagle, Dorothy, and Hilary Carnell, comp. *Oxford Literary Guide to the British Isles.* Oxford; Clarendon, 1977.
The first part of this guide is a listing of places in the British Isles associated with literary figures. Entries refer to maps at the end of the book and give descriptions of the events associated with the places. The second section is an index of authors, with a list of associated places.

282.   Fisher, Lois H. *A Literary Gazetteer of England.* New
       York: McGraw-Hill, 1980.
This gazetteer "is a comprehensive survey of the 'literary
associations' of more than 500 English (and occasionally
foreign) authors with more than 1,500 English localities."
Arrangement is alphabetical by place name. Entries include
both biographical and literary associations for that place.
An index by personal name aids access to information. An
excellent and attractive guide.

General Indexes, Abstracts, and Annual Bibliographies

283.   *Granger's Index to Poetry.* 8th ed. completely
       revised and enlarged, indexing anthologies
       published through June 30, 1985. Ed. by
       William F. Berhardt. New York: Columbia
       University Press, 1986. 1st ed., 1904; 2nd
       ed., 1918; 3rd. ed, 1940; 4th ed., 1958; 5th
       ed., 1962; 6th ed., 1973; 7th ed., 1982, with
       intervening supplements.
This series indexes anthologies of poetry. Each index
includes some anthologies from previous editions and some
new titles. Editions 1 through 3 also indexed prose
selections and are a useful guide to the contents of many
nineteenth century anthologies. Indexing by author, poem
title, first line, and subject.

284.   *Year's Work in English Studies.* Published for the
       English Association. London: Murray, 1921- .
       Annual.
These annual volumes feature bibliographic essays on
major books and articles on English and American
literature published in Europe, Britain, and America.
Arrangement is chronological, with indexing by author and
subject. Useful for its critical evaluation of literary work.

285. *MLA International Bibliography.* New York: Modern
      Language Association of America, 1921- .
      Annual. Title varies.
This annual bibliography has long been the basic source for
information on American publication in literary studies.
Arranged by language, nationality, period, and specific
author, it became easier to use in 1981, when a subject
index was introduced. Before 1981, subjects other than
author-as-subject were very difficult to find.
      Coverage has changed over the years: from 1921-
1955, only writings by Americans were listed; from
1956-1962, writers in countries and languages other
than English were included; from 1963 to the present,
when the title changed to the *MLA International
Bibliography,* coverage furthered widened.
      This index is now available on two different
databases and as a CD-ROM. The online version from
DIALOG extends back to 1964 and more retrospective
coverage is constantly being added. The database produced
by Wilsonline begins with January 1981. Their CD
version also goes back to 1981, with promise of further
coverage in the future.

286. *Annual Bibliography of English Language and
      Literature.* London: Modern Humanities
      Research Association, 1921- . Annual.
      Publisher varies.
This annual bibliography of English and American language
and literature includes books, pamphlets, and periodical
articles. The coverage is broad, including bibliographical
matters, scholarly method, language, literature and the
computer, and newspapers and other periodicals, as well as
the more usual language and literature topics. Indexed by
Author and Subjects, and by Scholars.

287. *Short Story Index: An Index to Stories in Collections and Periodicals.* New York: Wilson, 1953- .
This index lists short stories published in collections or in periodicals indexed in *Readers' Guide to Periodical Literature* and *Humanities Index* (see item 102). Annual, with five-year cumulations from 1900 to date.

288. *Abstracts of English Studies.* Calgary, Alta.: University of Calgary, 1958- .
This quarterly abstract gives concise descriptions of the contents of articles and monographs. About 500 journals dealing with American and English literature are covered. Arrangement is by country and then by period. An index appears quarterly, listed by names of people, names of anonymous works, and subjects treated. Annotations are descriptive.

289. *Linguistics and Language Behavior Abstracts: LLBA.* New York: Appleton, 1967- . Quarterly. Title varies. Publisher varies.
This index lists articles in all areas of linguistics and language study, including prosody. Arrangement is by author. It is searchable through DIALOG database 36 back to 1973 and on BRS file LLBA.

290. Howard-Hill, T.H. *Index to British Literary
      Bibliography.*   5 vols. Oxford: Clarendon
      press, 1969-1980.
The five volumes of this set include: Vol. 1, Bibliography of
British Literary Bibliographies; Vol. 2, Shakespearean
Bibliography and Textual Criticism.; Vol. 4, British
Bibliography and Textual Criticism: A Bibliography; Vol.
5, British Bibliography and Textual Criticism: A
bibliography (Authors); Vol. 6, British Literary
Bibliography and Textual Criticism, 1890-1969: An
Index. Volume 3 has not yet come out. The set "is intended
to cover books, substantial parts of books, and periodical
articles written in English and published in the English-
speaking Commonwealth and the United States after 1890,
on the bibliographical and textual examination of English
manuscripts, books, printing and publishing, and any
other books published in Great Britain or by British
authors from the establishment of printing in England."

Bibliographies of Bibliographies

291. Northup, Clark Sutherland. *A Register of
      Bibliographies of the English Language and
      Literature.* New York: Hafner Publishing,
      1925. Rept. 1962.
This bibliography is arranged in a general section and then
by individual authors and topics. Indexed. Useful for
identification of classic bibliographies of the Victorian
period, especially those found in periodicals.

292. Wortman, William A., ed. *A Guide to Serial Bibliographies for Modern Literatures.* New York: The Modern Language Association of America, 1982.
This guide is modelled on Richard Gray's *Serial Bibliographies in the Humanities and Social Sciences* (item 106). However, it focuses on materials of use to students of literature. It covers all nationalities and periods of literature, and bibliographies on both broad topics and specific authors. Entries are arranged topically and include a brief annotation. Very useful.

Periodicals

293. Ellegard, Alvar. *The Readership of the Periodical Press in Mid-Victorian Britain.* Stockholm: Almqvist & Wiksell, 1957.
This brief survey estimates the size, the class, the politics, and the religious views of the readership of various Victorian periodicals between 1860-1870. It covers newspapers, weekly reviews, other reviews (mainly quarterlies), monthly magazines, weekly journals, and magazines sold in weekly parts. Within these sections, arrangement is alphabetical by title. Index of titles covered. Extremely useful information, not superseded by later studies.

294. Boyle, Andrew. *An Index to the Annuals, 1820-1850.* Vol. 1; *The Authors (1820-1850).* Worcester: Andrew Boyle Ltd., 1967.
This author index to annuals and gift books published between 1820 and 1850 lists articles by the name signed to it. Pseudonyms are not identified. Some, but not all, initials are. Separate listings for "Author Of" signatures and anonymous works. A second volume on artists appearing in annuals during this period was projected but never published.

295.   Faxon, Frederick W. *Literary Annuals and Gift Books: A Bibliography, 1823-1903.* Reprinted with supplementary essays by Eleanore Jaimieson and Iain Bain. Pinner, Middlesex: Private Libraries Association, 1973.

Faxon's bibliography of annuals and gift books is reprinted with useful additional materials, including Jaimieson's essay on binding styles and Bain's on illustrations.

296.   Madden, Lionel, and Diana Dixon. *The Nineteenth-Century Periodical Press in Britain: A Bibliography of Modern Studies, 1901-1971.* New York: Garland, 1976.

This bibliography of studies of the nineteenth-century periodical press includes listings of books, pamphlets, periodical articles, dissertations, and theses appearing between 1901 and 1971. It includes sections on bibliographies, general history, individual periodicals and newspapers, and studies and memoirs of those connected with Victorian journals. Though it is not acknowledged in the book, this bibliography was previously published as a supplement to Volume 8 of *Victorian Periodicals Newsletter.* Contains many minor errors, so use with care.

297.   White, Robert B., Jr., ed. *The English Literary Journal to 1900: A Guide to Information Sources.* Detroit: Gale Research Company, 1977.

This bibliography lists English-language secondary sources and modern critical editions of pre-1900 British literary periodicals written since 1890. The book is well organized and indexed, with chapters on Bibliographies and Bibliographical Aids; General Studies; Periodicals; Persons; and Places, and indexes by Periodicals, Persons, and Places. The last year of full coverage is 1972, though scattered later items appear.

298. Patterson, Margaret. *Author Newsletters and Journals: An International Annotated Bibliography of Serial Publications Concerned with the Life and Works of Individual Authors.* Gale Information Guide Library. Detroit: Gale, 1979.
This guide lists publishing and bibliographic information on 1,129 serials on one author. It covers 435 authors from 28 countries. Arrangement is alphabetical by author, with cross references from pseudonyms. Seven appendixes list country, sponsoring institution, indexing and abstracting services, publishers, foreign terms, and sources consulted. Contents note on most entries.

299. Sullivan, Alvin, ed. *British Literary Magazines.* Vol. 3: *The Victorian and Edwardian Age, 1837-1913.* Westport, Conn.: Greenwood Press, 1984.
This volume is the Victorian and Edwardian section of a four-part reference guide to British literary magazines from 1698 to the mid-1980s. It covers 299 titles, 90 of which are discussed in essays and 209 which are listed in appendixes. Titles on which essays are written are selected on the basis of their importance to literary history and/or their revelation of the reading tastes of the period. Profiles of the magazines focus on their most important contributions or literary contents. A bibliography of sources and a publication history end each essay. Appendixes include a chronology, an index, and listings of the periodicals in the other volumes of the set, of nineteenth-century reviews concerned with foreign literature, of Victorian comic journals, of religious magazines with literary content, and of contributors. A rich and valuable source.

Bibliographies on British Writers

300. LeClaire, Lucien. *A General Analytical Bibliography of the Regional Novelists of the British Isles, 1800-1950.* Rev. ed. Collection d'histoire et littérature étrangères. Paris: Belles Lettres, 1969.
This analytical bibliography lists novels from the stated period and having a regional emphasis. Each entry includes a few biographical notes, the titles of novels of interest for regional studies, a listing of various editions of these works, and, wherever possible, the setting of each novel. Arrangement is chronological, with an index of authors' names and one of regions. Includes maps of the regions covered.

301. Watson, George, ed. *New Cambridge Bibliography of English Literature.* 5 vols. Cambridge: Cambridge University Press, 1969-1977.
Volume 3 of this set covers 1800-1900 and was the first volume published. Its cutoff date is 1968. It covers "literary authors native to or mainly resident in the British Isles." Entries include bibliographic entries on bibliographies, primary works, biographies, and criticism for both individual authors and broader topics, including socio-historical topics such as the education of women, history of the press, and sports. A shorter edition, *The Concise Cambridge Bibliography of English Literature, 600-1950* (2nd ed. Cambridge: Cambridge University Press, 1965), covers a shorter list of authors and singles out major works. An important source much in need of an update.

302. Watt, Ian P. *The British Novel: Scott through Hardy.* Goldentree Bibliographies in Language and Literature. Northbrook, Ill.: AHM Publishing, 1973.

This selected bibliography covers scholarship on the Victorian novel. Most of the citations are twentieth century, with a few classic works from the nineteenth. Chapters cover first broad topics and then individual authors. Indexed. Intended for advanced students.

303. Dyson, Anthony E., ed. *The English Novel: Select Bibliographical Guides.* Oxford: Oxford University Press, 1974.

This useful series of bibliographic essays covers the major authors of the traditional canon. Each essay is devoted to a different author and is by an expert in the field. Though it could obviously use updating, it is still useful for locating classic criticism and for its shrewd judgments about the problems of scholarship. Six of the twenty novelists covered are Victorians.

304. Wright, R. Glenn, comp. *Bibliography of English Language Fiction in the Library of Congress Through 1950.* Boston; G. K. Hall. *Author Bibliography . . .,* 8 vols., 1973. *Chronological Bibliography. . . ,* 8 vols. 1974. *Title Bibliography. . . ,* 9 vols, 1976.

This three-part bibliography is a valuable tool in bibliographical research. Each part is arranged geographically by the nationality of the author. Within a geographic designation, arrangement is, as appropriate to the section, alphabetical by author, title, or date. The introduction, basically the same in each set, contains information necessary to the effective use of the catalogs. Besides locating specific works, the volumes are useful for identifying pseudonymous authors, often with birth and death dates and place of birth.

305.   Altick, Richard D., and Andrew Wright. *Selective*
        Bibliography for the Study of English and
        American Literature. 6th ed. New York:
        Macmillan, 1979.
This bibliography is somewhat out-of-date, but it is still
useful for identifying important studies. The chapter on
"The Scope, Aims, and Methods of Literary Scholarship"
may be the definitive statement on this subject, and the
chapter "On the Use of Scholarly Tools" should be required
reading for all beginning literary researchers.

306.   Vinson, James, ed. *The Novel to 1900.* St. James
        Reference Library to English Literature.
        Chicago: St. James Press, 1985.
This series gives biocritical entries on both primary and
secondary authors. Each entry "consists of a biography, a
complete list of his published books, a selected list of
published bibliographies and critical studies on the
writer, and a signed critical essay on his work." Though
this volume contains information on pre-Victorian
writers, emphasis is on the Victorians.

Children's Literature

307.   Commire, Anne, ed. *Yesterday's Authors of Books*
        for Children: Facts and Pictures about Authors
        and Illustrators of Books for Young People from
        Early Times to 1960. 2 vols. Detroit: Gale,
        1977-78.
This set covers authors deceased before 1961. Each volume
covers authors and illustrators A to Z, with volume 2
having a cumulative index. Entries include biographical
information, a list of writings, quotations from the author,
and sources of further information. Well illustrated. Many
Victorian writers and artists are included. The set was
intended to continue and to cover a wide list of authors, but
no new volumes have been issued since 1978.

308. Carpenter, Humphrey, and Mari Prichard. *Oxford Companion to Children's Literature.* Oxford: Oxford University Press, 1984.

This Oxford Companion is typical in organization and treatment of its subject. Excellent short identifications of authors and works of children's literature, including many Victorian writers.

309. Nakamura, Joyce, ed. *Children's Authors and Illustrators: An Index to Biographical Dictionaries.* 4th ed. Detroit: Gale Research Company, 1986.

This index lists biographical sources of information on children's authors and illustrators. The biographies cited are generally brief; no book-length studies are listed. Victorian authors are generally well-served. Authors who have written some works for children, such as Ruskin, or works that are deemed suitable for children, such as Oscar Wilde, are included.

310. Helbig, Alethea K., and Agnes Regan Perkins. *Dictionary of British Children's Fiction: Books of Recognized Merit.* 2 vols. New York: Greenwood Press, 1989.

This dictionary lists in one alphabet characters, authors, and titles from children's fiction. Books have been selected for inclusion if they have been winners or finalists for major awards or if they appear on lists of recommended titles. Major writers and books of the Victorian period are listed if they are still read by children. This criterion means that Lewis Carroll, Ruskin, Kingsley, and Dickens are covered, but Charlotte Yonge, G. Manville Fenn, and other writers popular with Victorian children are not. Title entries give unusually clear and comprehensive plot summaries; author entries give brief biographical sketches; character entries describe the characters and their places within the novels. Excellent keyword index.

Literary Genres

311. *Victorian Detective Fiction: A Catalogue of the Collection Made by Dorothy Glover and Graham Greene.* Bibliographically arranged by Eric Osborne and introduced by John Carter. London: The Bodley Head, 1966.

This descriptive catalog of Victorian detective fiction is based on the private collection of Dorothy Glover and Graham Greene. It contains both books and serial fiction. The main part of the catalog is alphabetical by author, contains a bibliographic description of the item, the name of the detective, the Sadleir number, if in that collection, a note on the first publication, if not an original edition, and some additional notes as finding or identification aids. Indexes by detective, illustrator, and title.

312. Hubin, Allen J. *Crime Fiction, 1749-1980: A Comprehensive Bibliography.* New York: Garland, 1984.

This book is an updated, augmented, and corrected version of the author's 1979 *The Bibliography of Crime Fiction, 1749-1975.* The main section is alphabetical by author. Each entry includes author, author's dates when known, some references to further information on the author, titles of books, with date and publisher, setting and date, if not contemporary. Pseudonyms are identified. Indexes are by title, settings, series, and series character. A further index by date would increase its value for research on a particular period. Updated by 1981-85 supplement.

313. Albert, Walter. *Detective and Mystery Fiction: An International Bibliography of Secondary Sources.* Madison, In.: Brownstone Books, 1985.
This bibliography covers secondary sources on all periods and nationalities of mystery and detective fiction. The first section covers general reference works; the second historical and critical works on the genre as a whole. Section 3 covers dime novels, juvenile series, and pulps, and the last section covers individual authors. Entries are critical and descriptive. No period approach.

314. Buckley, J.A., and W.T. Williams. *A Guide to British Historical Fiction.* London: George G. Harrap, 1912.
This volume is arranged by the date of the subject of the novel. Only fiction concerning events in British history is listed. Entries include subject, title and author, and a brief indication of contents. Indexed by author.

315. Baker, Ernest A. *A Guide to Historical Fiction.* London: George Routledge & Sons, 1914.
This book lists historical novels. Arrangement is by country and then chronological, with brief annotations about the subject of the book.

316. Tymn, Marshall B., ed. *Horror Literature: A Core Collection and Reference Guide.* New York: Bowker, 1981.
This compilation of bibliographical essays covers horror literature during its various periods. Of interest to the Victorianist are the essays of Benjamin Franklin Fisher IV on "The Residual Gothic Impulse: 1824-1873" and of Jack Sullivan on "Psychological, Antiquarian, and Cosmic Horror: 1872-1919." Each essay is followed by a core collection list, with annotations giving plot highlights and evaluations of quality. Shorter sections cover verse and reference sources. Author and title index.

317. Bleiler, Everett F. *The Guide to Supernatural Fiction*. Kent, Ohio: Kent State University, 1983.
This volume covers all types of supernatural and occult fiction written between 1750 and 1960. The first section describes books and summarizes the stories. Brief critical evaluations are included. The indexes make the volume a useful reference source beyond its plot summary function. They include indexes of motifs and story types, an index of authors, and an index of titles. Victorian authors are well represented, though some authors who made only occasional forays into the supernatural are omitted.

318. Frank, Frederick S. *Guide to the Gothic: An Annotated Bibliography of Criticism*. Metuchen, N.J.: Scarecrow, 1984.
This bibliography cites secondary works on the Gothic in Britain, Canada, the U.S., France, and Germany, with brief coverage of other nations. The tradition is traced from its eighteenth century origins to modern times. Arrangement is by country and then chronological. A final section covers such special topics as the Gothic revival, vampires, artists, and actors.

319. Suvin, Darko. *Victorian Science Fiction in the UK: The Discourses of Knowledge and of Power*. Boston: G. K. Hall, 1983.
This book contains a bibliography of Victorian science fiction from 1848 to 1900, a biographical study of its writers, and an interpretive essay on the material in the bibliographical and biographical sections. The bibliography records first editions of English-language science fiction in book form published in or imported into the area comprising the present day United Kingdom between 1848 and 1900. The bibliography is chronological and includes brief annotations about the plot. The biographic section contains brief sketches on the writers of the books in the bibliographic section.

320. Sargent, Lyman Tower. *British and American Utopian Literature, 1516-1985: An Annotated, Chronological Bibliography.* New York: Garland, 1988.
This bibliography is a chronological list of English-language utopias published between 1516 and 1985. Brief annotations about contents. Author and title indexes.

Irish Literature

321. Brown, Stephen, J. *Ireland in Fiction: A Guide to Irish Novels, Tales, Romances, and Folk-Lore.* New Edition. Dublin: Maunsel, 1919.
This book is a list of English-language novels written in Ireland or dealing with Ireland or the Irish. The entries are arranged alphabetically by author and include notes on the subject of the book and critical opinions. Title and subject are indexed. Appendices on works of reference, publishers and series, classified lists by fiction types, and Irish fiction in periodicals.

322. Finneran, Richard L., ed. *Anglo-Irish Literature: A Review of Research.* New York: The Modern Language Association of American, 1976.
Recent Research on Anglo-Irish Writers. New York: Modern Language Association of America, 1983.
This collection of bibliographic essays is helpful in identifying editions, locations of manuscripts, important critical works, and other information essential to beginning scholarly research on Irish literature. For the Victorian scholar, James F. Kilroy covers sixteen writers in his section "Nineteenth-Century Writers." Ian Fletcher and John Stokes write on Oscar Wilde; Helmut E. Gerber discusses work on George Moore; and Stanley Weintraub covers Bernard Shaw. The supplement, *Recent Research on Anglo-Irish Writers,* covers work through 1981.

323. Kersnowski, Frank L., C.W. Spinks, and Laird
     Looms. *Bibliography of Modern Irish and Anglo-
     Irish Literature.* San Antonio, Texas: Trinity
     University Press, 1976.
This bibliography deals with Irish writers from 1880 to
the present. Arrangement is alphabetical by author.
Entries include author's dates, list of works, complete
works, bibliographies, biographical and critical studies.
The list of works includes books edited by the author,
introductions to other's works, and translations.

324. Harmon, Maurice. *Select Bibliography for the
     Study of Anglo-Irish Literature and Its
     Background: An Irish Studies Handbook.*
     Portmarnock, Ireland: Wolfhound Press, 1977.
This bibliography lists essential reference sources,
primary research materials, and a bibliography of
background reading for Irish literature. Though in need of
an update, it is especially useful for the wide variety of
background sources listed.

325. McKenna, Brian. *Irish Literature, 1800-1875: A
     Guide to Information Sources.* Detroit: Gale,
     1978.
     *Irish Literature, 1876-1950: A Guide to
     Information Sources.* Detroit: Gale, 1978.
These guides cover many more authors than Finneran's
Anglo-Irish Literature (item 322) but are less
authoritative in their critical evaluations. The first guide
contains one section devoted to "Background and Research"
and one to "Individual Authors." The second guide covers
anthologies, periodicals, bibliography, biography, and
criticism in the first three chapters. The fourth chapter
covers topics such as folklore and Irish history. The
remainder of the book lists works on individual authors.
Indexing in both volumes is excellent, with separate
author, title, and subject indexes.

326. Hogan, Robert, and others, eds. *Dictionary of Irish Literature.* Westport, Conn.: Greenwood Press, 1979.

The emphasis of this dictionary is biographical, though a few topical articles, such as the one on the Abbey Theatre, are included. An introduction and a lengthy opening essay on the history of Gaelic literature give a context for the biographical information in the body of the work. Entries include a basic outline of the author's life, a brief evaluation of his or her literary place and importance, and a listing of works by the author. A chronology, a bibliography, and an excellent index complete this introductory source.

327. Brady, Anne M., and Brian Cleeve. *A Biographical Dictionary of Irish Writers.* New York: St. Martin's Press, 1985.

This dictionary is a new edition of the *Dictionary of Irish Writers.* Entries include brief biographical information and a list of major works. No attempt is made to be bibliographically complete. Good for brief identifications.

Literature and Other Disciplines

328. *A Bibliography on the Relations of Literature and the Other Arts.* Hanover, N.H.: Dartmouth College, 1952- . Annual.

This topically arranged bibliography lists articles on literature and other arts in all modern periods and languages. Arrangement within topical sections is by period. No index.

329. *Literature and Society: A Selective Bibliography.*
Coral Gables, Fl.: University of Miami Press,
1956-67; 1950-55; 1956-60; 1961-65.
Annual listings,1966-74
This bibliography lists publications on the interrelations
of literature and society. Two sections, books and articles,
list items alphabetically by author. The cumulations have a
subject index, but the annual lists do not.

330. Dudley, Fred A. *Relations of Literature and Science:
A Selected Bibliography, 1930-1967.* Place
and publisher vary.
This bibliography lists books and articles on "the literary
impact of scientific thought." Arrangement is by period.
Indexed by author.

331. Kiell, Norman, ed. *Psychoanalysis, Psychology, and
Literature: A Bibliography.* 2 vols. 2nd ed.
Metuchen, N.J.: Scarecrow, 1981.
This guide focuses on articles and books dealing with a
psychological approach to literature and folklore.
Arrangement is topical; entries include bibliographic data
and no annotations. Subject index.

332. Natoli, Joseph, and Frederik L. Rusch, comp.
Psychocriticism: An Annotated Bibliography.
Bibliographies and Indexes in World Literature,
No. 1. Westport, Conn.: Greenwood, 1984.
This bibliography of psychocriticism is organized by
period and includes a chapter on the nineteenth century.
Within the chapter, there is a general section followed by
an alphabetic list by author discussed. The lists for each
author tend to be brief, because books and articles must
use "a fairly recognizable school or method of psychology."
Subject and author indexes.

333. Schatzberg, Walter, Ronald A. White, and Jonathan K. Johnson, eds. *The Relations of Literature and Science: An Annotated Bibliography of Scholarship, 1880-1980.* New York: Modern Language Association of America, 1987.
This annotated bibliography covers a hundred years of scholarship on the subject of the relationship between science and literature. Arrangement is chronological, beginning with a general section. From the seventeenth century on, coverage is by century. Each time period section is in two parts: Studies and Surveys and Individual Authors. Author index and subject index. Both books and periodical articles are listed. Foreign language sources, mostly European, are included. An excellent bibliography.

Serial and Sequence Fiction

334. Kerr, Elizabeth Margaret. *Bibliography of the Sequence Novels.* Minneapolis: The University of Minnesota Press, 1950.
This bibliography lists sequence novels, defined by the author as "a series of closely related novels that were originally published as separate, complete novels but that as a series form an artistic whole, unified by structure and themes that involve more than the recurrence of characters and some continuity of action." The largest section is on British and American novels. Many nineteenth century sequences.

335. Hicken, Marilyn E., comp. *Sequels.* 7th ed. London: Association of Assistant Librarians, 1982. Vol. I, Adult Books.
This bibliography lists books that have appeared as series, including some Victorian authors. Entries give name of series, titles of books in order of sequence. Dates of publication are given in some cases. Useful for deciding which Trollope novel to read first.

336. Vann, J. Don. *Victorian Novels in Serial.* New York: The Modern Language Association of America, 1985.

An interesting Introduction covers the history of serialization, its effects on authorship, and on the endings of parts. The body of the volume lists the serialized novels of sixteen Victorian novels. The place of publication, dates the parts appeared, and the chapters that appeared on each date are given for each entry. Notes appear at the end of some entries, giving information about such matters as date when the book appeared as a volume and peculiarities in the publishing history. An invaluable aid to studies on the serialization of the novel.

Speech and Rhetoric

337. Sutton, Roberta Biggs. *Speech Index: An Index to 259 Collections of World Famous Orations and Speeches for Various Occasions.* 4th ed. Revised and Enlarged. New York: Scarecrow, 1966.
Mitchell, Charity. *Speech Index: An Index to Collections of World Famous Orations and Speeches for Various Occasions.* 4th ed. Supplement, 1966-1980. Metuchen, N.J.: Scarecrow, 1982.

These indexes list speeches published in English between 1900-1965 and 1966-1980. Retrospective anthologies are included, so classic Victorian speeches can be found here. Entries are by author, subject, and type of speech.

338. Houlette, Forest. *Nineteenth-Century Rhetoric: An Enumerative Bibliography.* New York: Garland, 1989.

This bibliography covers primary and secondary works on rhetoric, composition, grammar, and the teaching of English between 1800 and 1920. It is in three parts: articles in books, articles in periodicals, and books. Entries are not annotated. Subject index.

Scottish   Literature

339. *Annual Bibliography of Scottish Literature.*
     Edinburgh: Scottish Group of the University,
     College, and Research Section of the Library
     Association, 1970- .
This supplement to the periodical *The Bibliotheck* is issued
annually and lists books, reviews, essays, and articles on
Scottish literature. The first supplement, published in
1970, covers work from 1969.

340. Aitken, William R. *Scottish Literature in English
     and Scots: A Guide to Information Sources.*
     Detroit: Gale, 1982.
This bibliographic guide to Scottish literature starts with
a section on general works and then proceeds
chronologically. The section covering 1800-1900 lists
bibliographies, literary histories and criticism,
anthologies, background studies, printing, publishing and
bookselling, periodicals, and other sources on a list of
individual authors. Some annotations.

341. Royle, Trevor. *Companion to Scottish Literature.*
     Detroit: Gale, 1983.
This dictionary of Scottish literature includes biographical
sketches of authors and important historians,
philosophers, and others who influenced Scottish
literature, principal literary works, institutions,
literary movements, historical events, printed ephemera,
and publishing. Biographical sketches include a listings of
the author's works and selected further references.

Victorian Literature

342. Sadleir, Michael. *Excursions in Victorian Bibliography.* London: Chaundy & Co., 1922.
This charming book is still a must for those interested in the bibliographic aspects of Victorian literature. The bibliographies of principle editions for the nine covered authors are valuable in identifying editions and the essays are informative and a delight to read.

343. Jones, Howard Mumford, and others. *Syllabus and Bibliography of Victorian Literature (Including the Regency Period).* Trial ed. 2 vols. Ann Arbor: Brumfield, 1934.
This syllabus leads the reader through a study of the literature of the nineteenth century. It is divided by five periods and each chronological period is in outline form. Bibliographic entries are grouped according to broad topics. Though obviously dated in its bibliographic information, the syllabus aspect still offers an interesting, structured approach to the study of the period.

344. Ehrsam, Theodore G., and Robert H. Deily, under the direction of Robert M. Smith. *Bibliographies of Twelve Victorian Authors.* New York: Wilson, 1936.
This classic bibliography examines over 200 sources and is still useful for extensive research. Arrangement is alphabetical by author criticized. Within each author section are a chronological outline, a section on bibliographic materials and one of biographical and critical material. Arrangement within these sections is alphabetical by critic. The lack of a subject arrangement or index can make the list somewhat laborious to use.

345. Templeman, William D., ed. *Bibliographies of Studies in Victorian Literature for the Thirteen Years, 1932-1944.* Urbana: University of Illinois Press, 1945
Wright, Austin, ed. *Bibliographies of Studies in Victorian Literature for the Ten Years 1945-1954.* Urbana: University of Illinois Press, 1956.
Slack, Robert C, ed. *Bibliographies of Studies in Victorian Literature for the Ten Years 1955-1964.* Urbana: University of Illinois Press, 1967.
Freeman, Ronald E., ed. *Bibliographies of Studies in Victorian Literature for the Ten Years 1965-1974.* New York: AMS Press, 1981
These bibliographies are reprints of those started in *Modern Philology* and continued in *Victorian Studies.* The first volume includes an index of the authors covered. The later volumes have indexes including the names of scholars, of the Victorian authors, and of general topics.

346. Sadleir, Michael. *XIX Century Fiction: A Bibliographical Record Based on His Own Collections.* 2 vols. London: Constable & Co., Ltd.; Berkeley: University of California Press, 1951.
This catalog to the private collection of Michael Sadleir is an invaluable guide to the nineteenth-century novel and its physical form. Minute physical descriptions and helpful warnings and notes make these volumes invaluable for both the collector and the editor.

347. Parrott, Thomas Marc, and Robert Bernard Martin. *Companion to Victorian Literature.* New York: Scribner's, 1955.
This books of essays provides brief historical, social, and biographical backgrounds for Victorian literature.

348. "Recent Studies in the Nineteenth Century" *Studies in English Literature, 1550-1900.* Autumn issue. 1961- .

This review of the year's scholarship in nineteenth century literary studies appears in the autumn issue of the journal. The review takes the form of a bibliographic essay noting significant titles and trends. Various scholars have written the essay over the years.

349. "Guide to the Year's Work in Victorian Poetry." *Victorian Poetry.* annual. 1963- .

Each year, since its first issue in 1963, *Victorian Poetry* has included in its Fall issue a bibliographic essay on the year's scholarship on Victorian poetry. The growth and increasing specialization in this field is evident: in 1963 R.C. Tobias wrote the entire essay, covering eight pages. In 1984, Tobias covered only general materials. Specialists wrote separate essays on major figures. The entire survey covered 53 pages. A valuable, scholarly source.

350. Fredeman, William E. *Pre-Raphaelitism: A Bibliocritical Study.* Cambridge, Mass.: Harvard University Press, 1965.

This guide to materials on Pre-Raphaelitism is still the starting point for research on this subject. It lists not only primary and secondary printed sources but also the manuscript holdings of public and private collections in North America and the United Kingdom.

351. Buckley, Jerome H. *Victorian Poets and Prose Writers.* New York: Appleton-Century-Crofts, 1966.

This bibliography lists English-language sources for Victorian literature and related subjects. Excellent basic list, though out of date.

352. Faverty, Frederic E. *The Victorian Poets: A Guide to Research.* 2nd ed. Cambridge, Mass.: Harvard University Press, 1968.

This guide consists of a series of bibliographic essays on Victorian poets and poetic schools. Extremely useful for its information on standard editions and important secondary literature, it is in need of an update, since it is complete only to the end of 1966.

353. DeLaura, David J. *Victorian Prose: A Guide to Research.* New York: The Modern Language Association of America, 1973.

This guide consists of bibliographic essays on major Victorian prose writers. It also includes, at shorter length, material on lesser figures. Like the other research guides sponsored by the MLA, an important source despite its age.

354. Ford, George H., ed. *Victorian Fiction: A Second Guide to Research.* New York: The Modern Language Association of America, 1978.

This guide updates Lionel Stevenson's *Victorian Fiction: A Guide to Research* (Cambridge, Mass.: Harvard University Press, 1966) but does not supersede it. Both volumes discuss the literature on Victorian fiction in a series of essays by authorities in the field. The second edition adds several authors, and the critics writing the essays are often different from those in the previous volume. Outstanding but in need of an update.

355. Vann, J. Don, and Rosemary T. Van Arsdel. *Victorian Periodicals: A Guide to Research.* New York: Modern Language Association of America. Vol. 1, 1978. Vol. 2, 1989.

This guide covers location, use, and bibliography of Victorian periodicals. Volume 1 is a general guide; volume 2 covers more specialized areas, including periodicals of the 1890s, publishers' archives, the radical and labour press, periodicals and art history, women's serials, religious periodicals, serialized novels in magazines, children's magazines, Scottish and Welsh periodicals.

356. Wilson, Harris W., and Diane Long Hoeveler. *English Prose and Criticism in the Nineteenth Century: A Guide to Information Sources.* Detroit: Gale Research, 1979.

This listing of primary and secondary works on Romantic and Victorian prose writers includes surveys, reference works, and background studies as well as works on individual authors. Entries include information on the author's principal prose works, collected works (including standard editions), letters, biographies, critical studies, and bibliographies. Frequent errors and omissions mar this work. DeLaura's *Victorian Prose* (entry number 353) covers similar ground and is far better.

357. Wolff, Robert Lee, comp. *Nineteenth-Century Fiction: A Bibliographical Catalogue Based on the Collection Formed by Robert Lee Wolff.* 5 vols. Edited by Katherine Bruner. New York: Garland, 1981-1985.

This catalog based on Wolff's private collection is, in many way, a supplement to Michael Sadleir's *XIX Century Fiction* (item 346). Where Sadleir provides a full description of an item in Wolff's collection, Wolff notes only variants or peculiarities of provenance. Full bibliographic descriptions and notes are provided for items not in Sadleir. This collection includes manuscripts. Wolff himself completed the first volume of this work before his death. Subsequent volumes were compiled from his files.

358. Scott-Kilvert, Ian, ed. *British Writers.* Edited under the auspices of the British Council. 8 vols. New York: Scribners, 1981.

Volumes IV to VI of this set cover major British writers from Wordsworth to Owen. The articles originally appeared as a series of pamphlets entitled *Writers and Their Works,* intended to provide an introduction to the works of major figures. Arrangement is chronological by the author's birth. The index volume is necessary to make the best use of the set. Entries include survey of writer's career, critical evaluation, and a selected bibliography.

359. Grimes, Janet, and Diva Daims, with the editorial assistance of Doris Robinson. *Novels in English by Women, 1891-1920: A Preliminary Checklist.* New York: Garland, 1981.

This bibliography lists 5,267 British and U.S. women authors; 306 anonymous novels are included. The first section is alphabetical by author, then by tltle. The second lists novels by pseudonymous or anonymous authors or by authors whose names conceal sex. The third lists unverified works. A title index for all three sections follows. A volume listing authors from 1781 to 1890 is mentioned in the Introduction as being forthcoming.

360. *Nineteenth-Century Literature Criticism.* Detroit: Gale, 1981- . Irregular.
This series excerpts criticism of authors who lived between 1800 and 1900. Criticism is drawn from both contemporary and modern sources. About 30 authors are covered per volume.

361. Bloom, Harold, ed. *The Critical Perspective.* Vol. 7: *Early Victorian;* Vol 8: *Mid-Victorian;* Vol 9: *Late Victorian.* The Chelsea House Library of Literary Criticism. New York: Chelsea House Publishers, 1988.
This set covers twentith-century criticism of English-language authors whose major work was written before 1904. Arrangement is chronological, with each volume arranged by the death date of the authors. Entries include a brief biography of the author followed by the texts of important critical essays. A list of further reading concludes each volume.

362. Mazzeno, Laurence W. *The Victorian Novel: An Annotated Bibliography.* Englewood Cliffs, N.J.: Salem Press, 1989.
This bibliography covers secondary works on thirteen Victorian novelists. The material listed is accessible to lower-division students and of limited use to more advanced scholars.

Women's Literature and Literary Criticism

363. Myers, Carol Fairbanks, ed. *Women in Literature: Criticism of the Seventies.* Metuchen, N.J.: Scarecrow, 1976.
More Women in Literature. 1979.
These volumes list critical and biographical books and articles by and about women authors from the sixth century B.C. to 1977. The material was published between 1970 and 1977 and includes work on women characters, feminist criticism, biographical studies, interviews, and selected book reviews. Organization is alphabetical by author discussed with a general section covering period, genre, and other overview literature. The first volume has an index of critics and editors; supplement not indexed.

364. Schwartz, Narda Lacy. *Articles on Women Writers, 1960-1975: A Bibliography.* Santa Barbara: ABC-Clio, 1977.
Articles on Women Writers, Volume 2, 1976-1984: A Bibliography. 1986.
These two volumes list secondary works on women writers. They are arranged alphabetically by writer. Both well-known and more obscure authors are included. Each volume includes an index by critic.

365. Daims, Diva, and Janet Grimes, with Doris
      Robinson. *Toward a Feminist Tradition: An
      Annotated Bibliography of Novels in English by
      Women, 1891-1920.* New York: Garland,
      1982.
This annotated bibliography lists 3,407 titles by 1,723
women authors. The novels are selected from *Novels in
English by Women* (item 359). "The principal idea
governing our selection of the novels was the
unconventional treatment of women characters which
focuses attention either on the efforts of women to control
their lives or on social attitudes and conditions functioning
as counterforces to that achievement." Annotations are
based on comments of reviewers of the period. Title index.

366. Humm, Maggie. *An Annotated Critical Bibliography
      of Feminist Criticism.* Boston: G.K. Hall, 1987.
This bibliography is a core-list of criticism exploring
theory, ideology, and culture from a feminist perspective.
Sections are on broad topics, such as: Theory and Sexual
Politics, Arts, and History. Brief annotations give some
idea of the contents of the book or article. The subject index
contains the heading "Victorian," under which are listed
articles devoted entirely to this period. However, the
heading is not exhaustive, and many items dealing with the
Victorians are not listed there. Also index of contributors.

367. Frost, Wendy, and Michele Valiquette. *Feminist
      Literary Criticism: A Bibliography of Journal
      Articles, 1975-1981.* New York: Garland,
      1988.
This bibliography lists periodical articles on all aspects of
literature approached through feminist literary theory.
Arrangement is first chronological, then by genre. Indexes
by subject, author/title, and authors of articles.

368. Schlueter, Paul, and June Schlueter, eds. *An Encyclopedia of British Women Writers.* New York: Garland, 1988.

This one-volume encyclopedia covers British women writers from the Middle Ages to the present. Brief biographical essays outline the author's life. Bibliographies listing works and chief critical writings follow. Articles are signed. Name and subject index.

369. Todd, Janet, ed. *Dictionary of British Women Writers.* London: Routledge, 1989.

This biographical dictionary covers 427 women writers from all periods of British literary history. Brief biographical articles are followed by a list of the authors' works and major secondary sources. The entries are generally not as complete as those in the Schlueter's *An Encyclopedia of British Women Writers* (item number 368), and the contributors to the two sources are largely the same. The *Encyclopedia* is therefore the stronger work for research purposes.

370. Boos, Florence, with Lynn Miller. *Bibliography of Women and Literature.* 2 vols. New York: Holmes & Meier, 1989. Vol. I: Articles and Books (1974-1978) by and about Women from 600 to 1975. Vol. II: Supplement. Articles and Books (1979-1981) by and about Women from 600 to 1975. Vol. III: 1981-1985 (forthcoming).

This bibliography is a compilation of three annual bibliographies issued by *Women and Literature,* 1976-1978, supplemented by "entries from the PMLA and Modern Language Research bibliographies for 1979-81." The arrangement is by nationality and then by period, with subdivisions for genre. A numerical code, explained in the introduction, is the key to comparisons across these divisions. The second volume includes indexing by writers, by author treated, and by genre for both volumes.

Biographical Sources

371. Allibone, S. Austin. *A Critical Dictionary of English
      Literature and British and American Authors
      Living and Deceased From the Earliest Accounts
      to the Latter Half of the Nineteenth Century.* 2
      vols., 2 vols. supplement. Philadelphia,
      Lippincott, 1899.
This biographical dictionary identifies British and
American writers. The amount of information given in each
entry varies greatly, from brief identification of writings
to four or five column biographical and critical appraisals.
Useful for identifying now forgotten authors.

372. Kunitz, Stanley J., and Howard Haycraft. *British
      Authors of the Nineteenth Century.* New York:
      Wilson, 1936.
The date on this classic biographical dictionary is no bar to
its usefulness. Insightful articles on authors major and
minor have not been equaled for conciseness, clarity of
information, and critical judgment.

373. Magill, Frank N., ed. *Cycylopedia of World Authors.*
      3 vols. Rev. ed. Englewood Cliffs, N.J.: Salem,
      1974.
This encyclopedia contains the biographies of 975 authors.
Emphasis is on European and American authors, with
United States and English authors covered most thoroughly.
Each entry lists the author's principal works, a brief
biographical/critical essay, and a short bibliography.

374. Havlice, Patricia P., ed. *Index to Literary
      Biography.* 2 vols. Metuchen, N.J.: Scarecrow,
      1975. 1st supplement, 1983, 2 vols.
This indexes 50 collective biographies of literary figures.
The supplement adds another 57 volumes published before
1969-81. Lists pseudonyms.

375. Vinson, James. *Great Writers of the English Language.* Vol. 1: Poets; Vol. 2: Novelists; Vol. 3: Dramatists. New York: St. Martin's, 1979.
These volumes include biographical, bibliographical, and critical information on English writers. Arrangement is alphabetical by author. Each entry includes a biography, a list of works, a critical bibliography, and a signed critical essay of up to two pages.

376. *Dictionary of Literary Biography.* Detroit: Gale.
  Vol. 18: *Victorian Novelists After 1885.* Ed. Ira B. Nadel and William E. Fredeman, 1983.
  Vol. 19: *British Poets, 1880-1914.* Ed. Donald E. Stanford, 1983.
  Vol 21: *Victorian Novelists Before 1885.* Ed. Ira B. Nadel and William E. Fredeman, 1984.
  Vol. 32: *Victorian Poets Before 1850.* Ed. William E. Fredeman and Ira B. Nadel, 1984.
  Vol. 35: *Victorian Poets Before 1850.* Ed. William E. Fredeman and Ira B. Nadel, 1985.
  Vol. 55: *Victorian Prose Writers Before 1867.* Ed. William B. Thesing, 1987.
  Vol. 57: *Victorian Prose Writers Before 1867.* Ed. William B. Thesing, 1987.
  Vol. 70: *British Mystery Writers, 1860-1919.* Ed. Bernard Benstock and Thomas F. Staley, 1988.
This series is organized by "topic, period, or genre," each volume devoted to authors having one of these aspects in common. The volumes listed above are those covering Victorian authors. Each entry gives a list of the author's works, a career biography tracing the author's development as a writer of the literature covered in that volume, a list of secondary sources, biographies, bibliographies, and the main repository for the author's papers. The biographical essays are long, up to 20 pages, and are signed. Because of the topical arrangement, authors may be covered more than once in the series.

377.   Beacham, Walton. *Research Guide to Biography and Criticism.* 2 vols. New York: Research Publishing, 1985.

This guide lists biographical and autobiographical sources for major English language authors of all periods. Arrangement is alphabetical by author, with a listing at the beginning of volume 1 by literary period. Thirty-five authors are listed under the "Victorian" period, though some, such as Jane Austen and Walter Scott, are more often considered Regency, and some, such as Joseph Conrad and Walter De La Mare, are Edwardians. Entries include: Author's Chronology, a selected bibliography of the author's works, and Overview of Biographical Sources, Autobiographical Sources, Overview of Critical Sources, Evaluation of Selected Criticism, Other Sources, and Selected Dictionaries and Encyclopedias.

378.   Vinson, James. ed. *The Romantic and Victorian Periods: Excluding the Novel.* St. James Reference Guide to English Literature. Chicago: St. James Press, 1985.

This volume gives biographical, bibliographical, and critical information on nineteenth century writers other than novelists. It is divided into two section: one on the Romantics and one on the Victorians.

Pseudonyms

379. Haynes, John Edward. *Pseudonyms of Authors Including Anonyms and Initialisms.* New York, 1882. Rept.; Detroit: Gale, 1969.
This book is an alphabetical list of pseudonyms, anonyms, and initialisms used by authors of many nationalities and periods. Emphasis is on English and American authors of the eighteenth and nineteenth centuries. Arrangement is alphabetical by the first letter of the name, including "a," "an," and "the." Entries give pseudonym, real name, first date of use of pseudonym when known, and birth and death dates.

380. Cushing, William. *Initials and Pseudonyms: A Dictionary of Literary Disguises.* New York: T.Y. Crowell & Co., 1885. 2nd series, 1888.
This alphabetic listing of initials and pseudonyms covers a long list of names. The second series is a supplement and both should be used. The two volumes are especially useful in identifying author's signatures, such as "A Lady," "His Daughter," or "His Uncle," not usually considered in lists of pseudonyms.

381. Halkett, Samuel, and John Laing. *A Dictionary of Anonymous and Pseudonymous Publications in the English Language.* 3rd rev. and enl. ed. John Horden, ed. Harlow, England: Longman, 1980.
Originally published as *A Dictionary of the Anonymous and Pseudonymous Literature of Great Britain,* by the late Samuel Halkett and the late John Laing. (Edinburgh: W. Paterson, 1882-1888), this book identifies the authors of pseudonymous and anonymous works. Entries give the author's name, size of the book, number of pages, publication date, and source of information.

Archives, Manuscripts, and Special Collections

382. Edmond, John Philip. *Catalogue of English Broadsides, 1505-1897.* N.P.: James L. Lindsay-Crawford, 1898. Rept. New York: Burt Franklin, 1968.

This catalog is a chronological listing of British broadsides in the private collection of James L. Lindsay-Crawford, a major collector of this type of material. The broadsides are in prose, with two explained exceptions, and are "written in English, Printed in some part of the British Empire, or have a bearing on English history or institutions." Entries include bibliographic description and often a brief note on contents. Includes a separate list of printers, publishers, and sellers. Indexed by title, author, subject, place names, and persons and events mentioned.

383. Metzdorf, Robert F. *The Tinker Library: A Bibliographical Catalogue of Books and Manuscripts Collected by Chauncy Brewster Tinker.* New Haven: The Yale University Library, 1959.

This catalog of the Tinker collection gives full bibliographic descriptions for the contents of this distinguished collection. Since it contains manuscripts, first editions, and reprinting of the works of many Victorian authors, it is useful not only as a guide to the collection but also as a checklist for collectors and historians. The notation style is somewhat idiosyncratic but is fully explained. Indexed.

384. Madden, David, and Richard Powers. *Writers' Revisions: An Annotated Bibliography of Articles and Books About Writers' Revisions and Their Comments on the Creative Process.* Metuchen, N.J.: Scarecrow, 1981.
Part one of this bibliography lists "Articles and Books About Writers' Revisions." The arrangement is alphabetical by author. Part two is "Writers Talk About the Creative Process." This section is indexed by genres, revision problems, scholars and titles of their articles, and books, names of writers and their works, names of writers and works revised. This book presents thorough coverage of this specialized topic.

385. Rosenbaum, Barbara, and Pamela White, comps. *Index of English Literary Manuscripts.* Volume IV, 1800-1900. London and New York: Mansell, 1982.
This index lists extant manuscripts of major British and Irish authors of the nineteenth century. The body of the book lists the manuscripts with a description of the contents. A list of facsimiles for covered authors is also included. Part 1 covers 23 authors from A to G; part 2 has yet to appear. These volumes will be a major resource when completed.

Dissertations

386. Altick, Richard, D., and William R. Matthews, comps. *Guide to Doctoral Dissertations in Victorian Literature, 1886-1958.* Urbana: University of Illinois Press, 1960.
This book lists dissertations dealing wholly or in part with British literature from 1837 to 1900. It includes European, English, and American dissertations.

387. Gabel, Gernot U., and Gisela R. Gabel, comps.
      Dissertations in English and American Literature: Theses Accepted by Austrian, French, and Swiss Universities, 1875-1970.
      Hamburg: Gernot Gable Verlag, 1977.
The contents of this list are arranged by period, then by author written about, then date, and finally alphabetically by the author of the dissertation. Author and subject index.

Maps and Geography

388. Mitchell, Sir Arthur, and C.G. Cash. *A Contribution to the Bibliography of Scottish Topography.* Edinburgh: Printed at the University Press for the Scottish Historical Society, 1917.
This bibliography lists books and articles on all aspects of Scottish topography. Two sections, on place and on subject, contain some duplicate entries. Excellent source of Victorian studies on this subject, including tours, volumes of views, and maps.

389. Edwards, Ruth Dudley. *An Atlas of Irish History.* London: Methuen, 1973.
This atlas covers Irish history from the Middle Ages to 1971. The maps are small, one-page, and accompanied by a lengthy text. Extensive cross references are included in the text. The index lists proper names only.

390. Hyde, Ralph. *Printed Maps of Victorian London, 1851-1900.* Folkestone, Kent: Dawson, 1975.
The main section of this book on Victorian maps is a catalog of every map "focused on the original limits of London during the given period." Order is chronological. An introductory essay discusses map making for this period.

391. Howgego, James L. *Printed Maps of London, Circa 1553-1850.* 2nd ed. Folkestone, England: Dawson, 1978.
This catalog lists maps of London printed up to 1850. It includes a General Introduction tracing the production of maps of London, including a section on mapping 1800-1850, a bibliography, an Introduction to the Catalogue, the catalog (in chronological order), and an index.

392.   Smith, David. *Antique Maps of the British Isles.*
       London: B.T. Batsford, 1982.
This book gives detailed descriptions of early maps,
including those of the early nineteenth century to about
1845. Special attention is given to the various issues of
maps as an aid in dating. Arrangement is by mapmaker.
Appendices include information on collections, dealers,
price, dating, societies, and identification and dating of
maps. Bibliography and index.

393.   Watt, Ian. *A Directory of U.K. Map Collections.* 2nd
       ed. Map Curators Group Publication No. 3.
       Kingston-Upon-Thames, Surrey: British
       Cartographic Society, 1985.
This guide to map collections is arranged in three sections:
The Map Collections of the Copyright Libraries; Other Map
collections; and Stop Presses. Entries under the
administrative or parent organization for the collection
include information on the person responsible for the
collection, address, telephone and telex numbers, hours,
and a brief note on the nature of the collection. Three
indexes, alphabetical, geographical, and keyword, provide
excellent access to the contents.

394.   Smith, David. *Victorian Maps of the British Isles.*
       London: Batsford, 1985.
This catalog lists topographical atlases published between
1837 and 1900. Listings are by the cartographer,
draughtsman, engraver, lithographer, or publisher
"customarily named by map dealers in identifying the maps
or under the heading most sensibly adopted for the
commonest states." Entries cover the map-maker's period
of activity, quotations from the maps, prospectuses or
advertising describing them, average dimensions, scale,
title, principal features, and various issues. Indexing
allows the user to find these entries by location mapped.
Handsomely illustrated.

395. Dunbar, Gary S. *This History of Modern Geography:
      An Annotated Bibliography of Selected Works.*
      New York: Garland, 1985.

This book covers sources for the history of geography from
the mid-eighteenth century to the present. Three sections,
General and Topical, Geography in Various Countries, and
Biographical works, contain entries giving the citation
with a short annotation on the contents. Author and subject
index.

Medicine and Health

396. Brown, G.H., comp. *Lives of the Fellows of the Royal College of Physicians in London, 1826-1925.* Vol. 6 of *The Roll of the Royal College of Physicians of London,* by William Munk. 2nd ed. rev. and enl. London: Royal College of Physicians of London, 1878-1984.
This biographical listing is often referred to as "Munk's roll" and is the basic source for information on Victorian physicians.

397. *Index-Catalogue of the Library of the Surgeon-General's Office of the United States Army.* Washington: Government Printing Office, 1880. 2nd series, 1896; 3rd series, 1918; 4th series 1936; 5th series, 1959.
This catalog lists a vast quantity of medical literature from all periods. Its early starting date makes it useful for identifying Victorian titles. Arrangement is alphabetical, with authors and subject interfiled.

398. Morton, Leslie T. *A Medical Bibliography (Garrison and Morton): An Annotated Check-list of Texts Illustrating the History of Medicine.* 4th ed. Aldershot, England: Gower Publishing, 1983.
This classic bibliography first appeared in 1943. This first edition was based on Fielding H. Garrison's 1912 *Index-Catalogue of the Library of the Surgeon General's Office* and its 1933 revision. The bibliography is arranged by subject and, within subject section, chronologically. Brief, authoritative annotations. Indexes of personal names and of subjects. The essential starting point for the history of medicine.

399.   Corsi, Pietro, and Paul Weindling. *Information Sources in the History of Science and Medicine.* London: Butterworths, 1983.
This series of bibliographic essays covers the growth and state of the history of medical science. Part I contains essays on the relationship of medicine and other disciplines and on the development and main themes of medical history. Part II covers research methods and sources. Part III deals with specific sciences. Part IV covers non-European science and medicine. The subject index leads to specific subjects but broader coverage by time period and nation is lacking.

400.   Erlen, Jonathan. *The History of the Health Care Sciences and Health Care, 1700-1980: A Selective Annotated Bibliography.* New York: Garland, 1984.
This bibliography of English-language books, dissertations, documents and articles on the history of health care through 1980 is limited to titles available through interlibrary loan, with the exception of some reference works. Biographical and autobiographical works are not included. Most entries include a brief annotation on the contents. Organization is alphabetical by subject headings drawn from the 1980 edition of the *Medical Subject Headings.* This arrangement offers some difficulties of use that could be covered by more cross references. Indexed by author.

Music

Research Guides

401. Matthew, James E. *The Literature of Music.* London: Elliot Stock, 1896.
This volume is a valuable guide to Victorian writing on music. Earlier musical writing is also included. Index.

402. Haydon, Glen. *Introduction to Musicology: A Survey of the Fields, Systematic and Historical, of Musical Knowledge and Research.* Chapel Hill: The University of North Carolina Press, 1941.
This survey of systematic and historical musicology includes sections on The Sources of Musical History and on problems and Methods of Historical Research in Music. Bibliography and index. A classic work.

403. Marco, Guy A., with the assistance of Sharon Paugh Ferris. *Information on Music: A Handbook of Reference Sources in European Languages.* 3 vols. Littleton, Co.: Libraries Unlimited, 1975-1984.
This guide to research and bibliography covers all kinds of Western music, with emphasis on serious classical music. Volume 3 covers sources on the United Kingdom. Sections include lists of dictionaries, sources of various kinds of musical information, biographical sources, guides to general sources such as lists and indexes, lists of music, and discographies.

404.   Marco, Guy A. *Opera: A Research and Information Guide.* New York: Garland, 1984.
This guide offers an overview of research sources, beginning with the most general and moving to the specific. Those interested specifically in opera in Victorian England will find the sections on individual operas and on opera in specific countries useful. Critical annotations. Indexed by author/title and by subject.

405.   Gänzl, Kurt. *The British Musical Theatre.* 2 vols. New York: Oxford University Press, 1986. Vol. 1   1865-1914.
This volume is a basic aid in any research into musical theater in Britain. Beginning with 1865-1867, the new and original works of that time period are described and discussed. The narrative section is followed by a listing of the productions discussed, with information on details of the original production, on other productions and revivals, touring dates, and cast lists. Yearly coverage begins with 1870. Appendices in volume one list printed music and recorded music from musicals discussed in the body of the work. No indexing.

406.   Duckles, Vincent H., and Michael A. Keller. *Music Reference and Research Materials: An Annotated Bibliography.* 4th ed. New York: Schirmer Books; London: Collier Macmillan, 1988.
This list of reference and research materials covers a broad range of general and specialized sources on music. Chapters are organized by the type of reference covered ("Histories and Chronologies," "Bibliographies of Music Literature"). Entries are annotated. Indexed by authors, editors, and reviews, by subject, and by title. Excellent starting point.

Dictionaries and Encyclopedias

407. Sadie, Stanley, ed. *The New Grove Dictionary of Music and Musicians.* 2 vols. Washington, D.C.: Grove's Dictionaries of Music, 1980.
This dictionary is based on *Grove's Dictionary of Music and Musicians,* but most of its material is new. It covers a wide range of music and musical traditions, including folk and non-Western music. For the Victorianist, the old 5th edition of Grove is still useful, because its emphasis is on the nineteenth century. The *New Grove* is, however, invaluable for the currency of its scholarship and its coverage of composers, performers, others within the musical world, terminology, genres, forms, and many other musical matters. Longer articles are signed and include bibliographies.

408. Arnold, Denis, ed. *The New Oxford Companion to Music.* 2 vols. Oxford: Oxford University Press, 1983.
This *Oxford Companion* provides both short definitions and longer articles on all aspects of music. Bibliographies are included where appropriate.

409. Bohle, Bruce, ed. *International Cyclopedia of Music and Musicians.* 11th ed. New York: Dodd, Mead, 1985.
This volume encyclopedia covers all aspects, periods, and nationalities of music and musicians. It has both short identifications and longer articles on major figures and topics. Biographical articles include a listing of works.

410. Randel, Don Michael. *The New Harvard Dictionary of Music.* Cambridge, Mass.: Belknap Press of Harvard University Press, 1986.
This dictionary gives definitions of musical terms ranging from one line to several pages. Longer articles have bibliographies. The overview articles on the music of various nations are especially good. Biographical articles are not included.

Chronologies

411. Hall, Charles J, comp. *A Nineteenth-Century Musical Chronicle: Events, 1800-1899.* Music Reference Collection. Westport, Conn.: Greenwood, 1989.
This chronology is the second of three planned volumes to cover events in music since 1750. Though there are some facts omitted that might have reasonably been included, this is the best source for this type of information for those interested in the nineteenth century. Excellent index.

Indexes

412. *The Music Index: A Subject-Author Guide to Music Periodical Literature.* Warren, Mich.: Harmonie Park Press, 1949- . Monthly.
This index lists authors, proper names, and subjects found in the music periodical literature. Reviews of books, music, performances, and recordings are listed under the headings "Book Reviews," "Works," name of the performer, and "Recordings."

413. *RILM: Répertoire International de Littérature Musicale.* New York: International Musicological Society, 1967- . Quarterly, with annual cumulations.

This annual abstract of international musical literature is arranged by broad topics. Abstracts are descriptive of contents. Author index in monthly parts; annual author-subject index. Its greatest disadvantage as a scholarly tool is that it runs about five years behind current date on its indexing. Searchable online back to 1972 as DIALOG file 97.

414. *Bibliographic Guide to Music.* Boston: G.K. Hall, 1974- . Annual.

These annual subject listings are based on the catalog of The Research Libraries of The New York Public Library plus entries from the Library of Congress MARC tapes. Coverage is from September of the year before the date of the volume to August of the listed year.

415. Wenk, Arthur B. *Analyses of Nineteenth and Twentieth-Century Music.* Index and Bibliography Series, No. 25. Boston, Mass.: Music Library Association, 1987.

This volume indexes periodicals, monographs, Festschriften, and dissertations containing technical analyses of modern music. Arrangement is alphabetical by composer and includes an index of authors. Entries include citation, a note of the musical work covered, and the composer's dates when not mentioned in the article title.

Bibliographies

416. Gooch, Bryan N.S., and David S. Thatcher. *Musical Settings of Late Victorian and Modern British Literature: A Catalogue.* New York: Garland, 1976.

This volume is a companion to Gooch and Thatcher's *Musical Settings of Early and Mid-Victorian Literature* (see item 417). Arrangement is the same, but only author and composer indexes are included in this volume. The authors covered here were born after 1840 and lived till 1900 or later.

417. Gooch, Bryan N.S., and David S. Thatcher. *Musical Settings of Early and Mid-Victorian Literature: A Catalogue.* New York: Garland, 1979.

This catalog lists "published and unpublished settings of texts by prominent British authors who were, for the most part, born after 1800 and who lived to 1850 or later." The main part of the catalog is arranged by author. Entries include author's names and dates, the title of the literary work, first line if a poem, form if other than a poem, name of book or periodical of first publication, and date of first publication. An entry number is listed, followed by composer of setting, variant title of setting, publication details of setting, title of collection in which it appeared, place of publication, name of publisher, and date of publication. A series of abbreviations indicate form, vocal specifications, and accompaniment required. Entries may include additional information about the setting. Indexed by author, composer, and title/first line. See also item 416.

418.   Senelick, Laurence, David F. Cheshire, and Ulrich
       Schneider. *British Music-Hall, 1840-1923: A*
       Bibliography and Guide to Sources, with a
       Supplement on European Music-Hall. Hamden,
       Conn.: Archon Books, 1981.
This bibliography lists books, records, and articles on the
British music hall. Sections are topical, from General
Reference to Recordings, with alphabetical arrangement
within sections. Especially useful is the section on
individual regions and specific music halls. Some
annotations. Index by authors and by London music halls.

419.   Farkas, Andrew. *Opera and Concert Singers: An*
       Annotated International Bibliography of Books
       and Pamphlets. New York: Garland, 1985.
This bibliography lists monographs by and about vocalists
having a stage or concert career. 796 singers are covered,
many of whom worked during the nineteenth century. Many
items have contents annotations. A useful guide to
otherwise difficult-to-find material, but not, as the
author emphasizes, exhaustive.

Dissertations

420.   Hewitt, Helen, comp. *Doctoral Dissertations in*
       Musicology. 4th ed. Philadelphia: American
       Musicological Society, 1965.
This list of American and Canadian dissertations in the field
of musicology is arranged topically, with the largest
section by period.

Library Catalogs

421. *The Catalogue of Printed Music in the British Library to 1980.* 62 vols. London: Saur, 1981-1987.
This catalog includes musical texts of all kinds arranged alphabetically by main entry. It gives in a single sequence the information in the various earlier catalogs of the British Library collections.

422. *The British Catalogue of Music, 1957-1985.* New York: Saur, 1987- .
This set is a cumulation of 29 annual volumes of music holdings of the British Library. The original catalogs are edited to provide standard headings and three indexes arranged by Coates classification code, subject, and composer and title. The complete set will be ten volumes.

Museums and Collections

423. Coover, James. *Musical Instrument Collections: Catalogues and Cognate Literature.* Detroit: Information Coordinators, 1981.
This bibliography lists catalogs, inventories, guides, articles, and other literature that list musical instrument collections and exhibitions. The book is divided into two parts: Institutions and Expositions, and Private Collections. Each section has its own guide to entries. Part I is listed by the city in which the display or collection is located. Part II is by the owner of the collection. Appendices Include a chronological list of expositions and exhibitions, 1818-1978. Many nineteenth-century exhibits are listed.

Biography

424. Brown, James D., and Stephen S. Stratton. *British Musical Biography: A Dictionary of Musical Artists, Authors, and Composers Born in Britain and Its Colonies.* Birmingham: S.S. Stratton, 1897.
This biographical dictionary covers British composers, musicians, and lyricists of all periods. Entries are short and contain a list of works.

425. Baker, Theodore. *Baker's Biographical Dictionary of Musicians.* 7th ed. Revised by Nicolas Slonimsky. New York: Schirmer Books; London: Collier Macmillan, 1984.
This excellent, one-volume dictionary contains biographies of composers and musicians of all countries and periods. Biographies of major figures include bibliographies.

Painting, Engraving, Sculpture, and Illustration

Research Guides

426. Ehresmann, Donald L. *Fine Arts: A Bibliographic Guide to Basic Reference Works, Histories, and Handbooks.* 2nd ed. Littleton, CO.: Libraries Unlimited, 1979.

This guide incorporates, expands, and updates Mary Chamberlin's *Guide to Art Reference Works* (Chicago: American Library Association, 1959). It covers general works on art research rather than more specialized guides on specific topics. The cutoff date is September 1, 1978. Annotated. Author, title, subject index.

427. Arntzen, Etta, and Robert Rainwater. *Guide to the Literature of Art History.* Chicago: American Library Association; London: The Art Book company, 1980.

This guide is addressed to the advanced researcher in art history. It covers all fields and countries. Arrangement is by medium, then by geographic location. Annotations to entries are evaluative. The cut-off date is 1977. An excellent, comprehensive work, only in need of update.

428. Brenni, Vito J., ed. *Book Illustration and Decoration: A Guide to Research.* Westport, Conn.: Greenwood Press, 1980.

This guide to research covers the extensive literature on book illustration of all periods and countries. Chapter 6 approaches the subject by individual countries, chapter 5 by period. Entries are not annotated. Author and subject indexes.

429. Jones, Lois Swan. *Art Research Methods and
      Resources: A Guide to Finding Art Information.*
      2nd ed., revised and enlarged. Dubuque:
      Kendall/Hunt, 1984.
This guide to research begins with "Defining the Study" and
proceeds from general to specialized reference sources.
Libraries and research centers of interest to art
researchers are described, and information on seldom-
covered aspects of research, such as finding single titles in
a series, is covered. An unusually thorough guide, useful at
all levels and stages of research.

430. Pollard, Elizabeth B. *Visual Arts Research: A
      Handbook.* New York: Greenwood Press, 1986.
This guide to research covers art research tools and
methods in nine chapters. The book begins with an
overview of the research process and a second chapter on
the organization of collections in libraries. The emphasis
is on the types of materials needed by college art students.
Sections are in the form of bibliographic essays. Online
database searching is discussed. Indexed by author, title,
and some general topics. A good guide for beginners.

Dictionaries and Encyclopedias

431. Williamson, George C. *Bryan's Dictionary of
      Painters and Engravers.* New edition, revised
      and enlarged. New York: Macmillan, 1903.
Bryan's Dictionary first appeared in 1816 and for more
than a century has been considered the standard work in
this field. Revision followed in 1849, a supplement in
1876, and another revision in 1884. The 1903 revision
expanded to five volumes. Arrangement is alphabetical.
Entries vary in length depending on the importance and
productivity of the artist. Major biographical facts, major
works, and positions held are all included. Black and white
plates included. The final volume includes a useful section
on "Monograms of Painters and Engravers."

432. Grant, Maurice Harold. *A Dictionary of British Sculptors: From the XIIIth Century to the XXth Century.* London: Rockcliff Publishing, 1953.
This dictionary gives brief information about British sculptors. Some identifications are no longer than one line; others run about one page. Indexed by sitters and titles of sculptures.

433. *Encyclopedia of World Art/Enciclopedia Universale dell'Arte.* 15 vols. and supplement. New York: McGraw-hill; Venezia: Instituto per la Collaborazione Culturale, 1959.
This monumental encyclopedia covers all aspects and nationalities in the visual arts, including architecture. Each volume is roughly half articles, with some line drawings accompanying and illustrating the articles, and half plates keyed to the articles in the volume. The 15th volume contains an index to the set. The supplement updates to 1983 scholarly commentary and bibliographies. Excellent articles.

434. Myers, Bernard S., ed. *McGraw-Hill Dictionary of Art.* 5 vols. New York: McGraw-Hill, 1969.
This dictionary has many lengthy articles as well as brief identifications and definitions. It covers terms, artists, art works, movements and schools, techniques, associations, and national art. Many illustrations. No index.

435. Osborne, Harold, ed. *Oxford Companion to Art.* Oxford: Clarendon, 1970.
This volume is in the format of all of the Oxford Companions. Short, alphabetically-arranged articles provide an introduction to the fine arts for the non-specialist. All countries and times are covered. Numbers at the ends of entries refer the user to entries in the bibliography at the end of the book.

436. Mallalieu, H.L. *The Dictionary of British Watercolour Artists Up to 1920.* N.P.: Antique Collectors' Club, 1976.
This dictionary covers 6000 British watercolor artists of all periods. Entries are brief and include, when possible, sources for further study and museums in which examples of work may be found.

437. Wood, Christopher. *Dictionary of Victorian Painters.* Research by Christopher Newall. 2nd ed. rev. and enl. Woodbridge, England: Antique Collectors Club, 1978.
This dictionary gives brief identifications of Victorian painters, an estimate of the monetary value of their works, and a bibliography for each artist. The second part of the work has reproductions in black and white of paintings. An index lists artists' monograms.

438. Engen, Rodney, K. *Dictionary of Victorian Engravers, Print Publishers and Their Works.* Cambridge: Chadwyck-Healey: Teaneck, N.J.: Somerset House, 1979.
This dictionary is divided into two parts: Part I lists engravers: Part II lists the publishers, printers, and printsellers of engravings. Entries on engravers give brief biographical information and an account of the career. Important works are listed. A list of sources of information is given at the end of each entry.

439. Murray, Peter, and Linda Murray. *The Penguin Dictionary of Art and Artists.* 5th ed. Harmondsworth, England: Penguin, 1983.
This dictionary contains short definitions and articles on Western art from 1300 to the present. Material covered includes technical terms, schools, and individual artists. A handy source for quick answers and general background.

440. Engen, Rodney. *Dictionary of Victorian Wood Engravers.* Cambridge: Chadwyck-Healey, 1985.
This dictionary lists wood engravers, draughtsmen who worked on wood, and engraving firms of Victorian Britain. Entries list name, dates of working life, a statement about the artist's importance, biographical information, addresses, a selected list of engraved works, a discussion of work methods, critical assessment by critics with references for further research, honors, place and date of death, select list of works in collections examined, and the engraver's signature. An impressive work.

Genres and Subjects

441. Pavière, Sydney. *Dictionary of Victorian Landscape Painters.* Leigh-on-Sea, England: F. Lewis, 1968.
This dictionary gives brief identifications of a large number of landscape painters of the Victorian period. Entries give, to the extent possible, dates, locality, training, collections containing the artist's work, exhibitions in which the artist appeared, sources of reproductions, and a bibliography. Black and white reproductions.

442. Daniel, Howard. *Encyclopaedia of Themes and Subjects in Painting.* London: Thames and Hudson, 1971.
This book gives short versions of the stories of many common themes and subjects in European painting from the early Renaissance to the mid-nineteenth century. The majority of the entries cover biblical stories, saints' lives, and myth. Useful for students unfamiliar with such material.

443.   Wilson, Arnold. *A Dictionary of British Military Painters.* Leigh-on-Sea, England: F. Lewis, 1972.

This dictionary covers British artists "whose main output is military in nature." Brief entries include name, dates, some biographical information, published sources of paintings, exhibitions, and sources of information. Black and white reproductions of the works of some of the discussed painters are in a section at the end of the book.

444.   Lewis, Frank. *A Dictionary of British Bird Painters.* Leigh-on-Sea, England: F. Lewis, 1974.

This dictionary covers British artists who painted birds from the seventeenth century to 1974. Entries give names, dates, some brief biographical information, exhibits, and reproductions. Black and white reproductions are in a group at the end of the book.

445.   Sartin, Stephan. *A Dictionary of British Narrative Painters.* Leigh-on-Sea, England: F. Lewis, 1978.

This dictionary lists British narrative painters of all periods. Entries give dates, subjects painted, exhibitions, names of major works, and some biographical information. Black and white reproductions end the book.

446.   Hook, Philip, and Mark Poltimore, eds. *Popular Nineteenth-Century Painting: A Dictionary of European Genre Painters.* Woodbridge, England: Antique Collectors Club, 1986.

This book lists and reproduces by subject, in color or black and white nineteenth-century paintings of Western Europe. Though its focus goes beyond Britain, it is a useful beginning for those interested in the subjects used by artists in genre paintings and in popular art. A general introduction precedes the reproductions and each subject section is given a brief introduction.

Illustration and Illustrators

447. Ray, Gordon N. *The Illustrator and the Book in England from 1790 to 1914.* New York: Oxford University Press; New York: Pierpont Morgan Library, 1976.

This catalog lists in chronological order major illustrators from 1790 to 1914. Entries on individual artists give a brief biography followed by a list of illustrated books with bibliographic description. Brief annotations list distinctive features about the illustrations. Topical essays, such as "Engraving on Copper" and "Other Artists Who Drew for Wood Engravers," deal with various aspects of illustration from this period and list artists not included in other sections. Index of artists and of authors and titles.

448. Baker, Charles, ed. *Bibliography of British Book Illustrators, 1860-1900.* Birmingham, England: Birmingham Bookshop, 1978.

This bibliography lists works illustrated by British artists between 1860 and 1900. Listings are by illustrator and then by author. Entries include: title, date of first edition, publisher, series, number of illustrations, number of full page illustrations, the format, and, where possible, a description of the covers. Author/title index. Handsomely illustrated and a pleasure to use.

449. Olmstead, Charles, and Jeffrey Egan. *Victorian Novel Illustration: A Selective Checklist, 1900-1976.* New York: Garland, 1979.

This bibliography is an annotated list of books and articles on British novel illustration during the Victorian period. Arrangement is chronological, with an index of authors and a general index covering book titles, illustrators, and authors of illustrated novels.

450.   Houfe, Simon. *The Dictionary of British Book Illustrators and Caricaturists, 1800-1914.* Revised. Woodbridge, Suffolk: Antique Collectors Club, 1981.

The beautifully illustrated volume covers the history and biography of the nineteenth and early twentieth century British illustrator's art. Eleven chapters at the beginning cover the history and development of illustration during this period. The biographical dictionary follows. Appendixes give schools and specialists. A listing of artists' monograms, a bibliography, and an index complete the volume.

Exhibitions

451.   Graves, Algernon. *The British Institution, 1806-1867: A Complete Dictionary of Contributors and Their Work From the Foundation of the Institution.* Bath: Kingsmead Reprints, 1967. Rept. 1875 ed.

This alphabetical listing of artists covers those who exhibited their works at the British Institution from its founding in 1806 through 1867. The list is drawn from the catalogs of these exhibitions and anonymous entries are not identified. Entries up to 1852 give the size of the work measured from the outsides of the frames. From 1852 on, sizes are not given, but the price asked by the artist is.

452.   Graves, Algernon. *A Dictionary of Artists Who Have Exhibited Works in the Principal London Exhibitions From 1760 to 1893.* 3rd ed. with additions and corrections. Bath: Kingsmead Reprints, 1970. Rept. 1901 ed.

This work might better be called a list than a dictionary. Entries list name of artist, town, first and last year of exhibition, speciality, and number of appearances at various recurring exhibitions.

453. Graves, Algernon. *The Royal Academy of Arts: A Complete Dictionary of Contributors and Their Work From Its Foundation in 1769 to 1904.* New York: Burt Franklin, 1972. Rept. 1905-06 ed.

This listing, drawn from the catalogs of the Royal Academy Exhibitions, gives the name of the artist, type of art practiced, address, and a list of works exhibited arranged by date.

454. Graves, Algernon. *A Century of Loan Exhibition, 1813-1912.* 5 vols. New York: Burt Franklin, 1913.

This set is an alphabetical listing by artists of "the most important public exhibitions during that period in London and the provinces." Part way through the project, Edinburgh and Glasgow were added. Each entry includes the artist's name and dates, the place of exhibition, date of exhibition, title of painting, and the owner of the painting. The set is indexed by portraits and by owner.

455. Rinder, Frank, comp. *The Royal Scottish Academy, 1826-1916.* Bath: Kingsmead Reprints, 1975. Rept. 1917 ed.

This catalog lists members of the Royal Scottish Academy for the listed dates, a catalog of works exhibited during this period, lenders, donors, and bequeathers of exhibited works, place names, and important architectural subjects.

456.   Johnson, Jane, comp. *Works Exhibited at The Royal
        Society of British Artists, 1824-1893.* N.p.:
        Antique Collectors' Club, 1975.
This work is intended to complement Algernon Graves' lists
of exhibitors at the Royal Academy and at the British
Institution. It lists both members and non-members who
exhibited at the Society between 1824 and 1893.
Information was compiled from the catalog of the shows.
Arrangement is alphabetical by artist, with works by
individual artist listed chronologically. Medium, price, and
catalog number are given for each art work. It also
includes a list of members of the New English Art Club
from 1888 to 1917. No indexing.

Museums and Collections

457.   Blunt, Anthony, and Margaret Whinney. *The
        Nation's Pictures: A Guide to the Chief National
        and Municipal Picture Galleries of England,
        Scotland, and Wales.* London: Chatto and Windus,
        1950.
This guide lists major collections of paintings in Great
Britain. Descriptions of collections run from three to
thirty-five pages.

Sales Catalogs and Prices

458.   Graves, Algernon. *Art Sales From Early in the
        Eighteenth Century to Early in the Twentieth
        Century.* 3 vols. New York: Burt Franklin,
        1970. Reprt. 1918-21 ed.
These volumes attempt to give the date, auctioneer, owner,
lot number and title of the picture, purchaser and sale
price for 200 years of art sales in Britain. Invaluable
until the Getty *Index of Paintings Sold in the British Isles
During the Nineteenth Century* (item 461) is completed.

459. *Sotheby & Company Catalogues of Sales.* Ann Arbor, Mich.: Xerox University Microfilms, 1973. Part I, 1734-1850 (71 reels); Part II, 1851-1900 (148 reels).

This collection of Sotheby & Company's auction catalogs contains information of interest to those in art history, numismatists, historians of drama and theater, and social historians. Access is through *Sotheby and Co. Catalogue of Sales: A Guide to the Microfilm Collection* (Ann Arbor: University Microfilms, 1973). A separate guide exists for each part.

460. Nahum, Peter, ed. *Prices of Victorian Paintings, Drawings, and Watercolours From the Records of Sotheby's Belgravia.* London: Carter Nash Cameron Limited, 1976.

This volume lists in two sections, oil paintings and watercolors, the prices brought by Victorian paintings at Sotheby's Belgravia between 1971 and 1975. Arrangement is alphabetical by artist, then by date of sale. Drawings are included in the watercolor section.

461. Fredericksen, Burton B., assisted by Julie I.
      Armstrong and Doris A. Mendenhall. *The Index
      of Paintings Sold in the British Isles During the
      Nineteenth Century.* Vol. 1, 1801-1805. Santa
      Barbara: ABC-Clio, 1988.
This project, sponsored by the Getty Museum, though not
now covering the Victorian period, will eventually trace
the provenance of a huge number of the works of art sold
during the nineteenth century. This volume is the first of a
twenty-volume set listing information from auction
catalogs, sales by private contract, and pictures sold in
book sales. Data drawn from sales catalogs greatly expands
the information available in Algernon Graves' *Art Sales
From Early in the Eighteenth Century to Early in the
Twentieth Century* (item 458). Arrangement is
chronological. Information includes dates of sale,
auctioneer's name, location of sale, seller's name, source
for the name, size of the sale, locations of extant catalogs,
annotations, and other useful comments. Indexes allow
access by catalog, paintings, and owners. No automated
access is now available, but Frederickson hopes that such
access will be provided later in the project.

Women   Artists

462. Women's History Research Center. *Female Artists
      Past and Present.* New ed. Berkeley: Women's
      History Research Center, 1974. Supplement,
      1975
Though the emphasis of these volumes is on currently
practicing women artists, both volumes begin with a
section "Female Artists in Art History." An alphabetical
list briefly identifies the artist and gives sources of
further information.

463. Bachmann, Donna G., and Sherry Piland. *Women Artists: An Historical, Contemporary, and Feminist Bibliography.* Metuchen, N.J.: Scarecrow, 1978.

This bibliography of works on European, British, and American women artists is arranged chronologically. The section on the nineteenth century includes many Victorians. Names are arranged alphabetically. Entries include brief biographical information and a list of sources. Some bibliographic entries are annotated. Good source for information on some neglected artists.

464. Yeldham, Charlotte. *Women Artists in Nineteenth-Century France and England: Their Art Education, Exhibition Opportunities and Membership of Exhibiting Societies and Academies, with an Assessment of the Subject Matter of Their Work and Summary Biographies.* 2 vols. New York: Garland, 1984.

This title makes description unnecessary. It is a reprint of a PhD thesis for the Courtauld Institute and is both descriptive of the art world and art education of the nineteenth century and biographical. It brings together much hard-to-find information, including lists and descriptions of exhibitions showing the works of women artists and a section on societies of women artists. Much material for further study here.

465. Pettys, Chris, and others. *Dictionary of Women Artists: An International Dictionary of Women Artists Born Before 1900.* Boston: G. K. Hall, 1985.
This international dictionary includes more than 21,000 women artists, sculptors, printmakers, and illustrators born before 1900. It does not include photographers, architects, craftswomen, and designers unless they are also associated with the represented art forms. Each entry attempts to include name, including maiden and/or married name, pseudonyms, dates and places of birth and death, media and subject matter, place of residence and activity, identification of other artists in family, schools and teachers, exhibition record, and bibliographical references. Includes excellent cross-references.

466. Dunford, Penny. *A Biographical Dictionary of Women Artists in Europe and America Since 1850.* Philadelphia: University of Pennsylvania Press, 1989.
This dictionary gives brief biographical and critical information on women artists since 1850. A list of places where the artist's works may be seen in included in each entry. Includes black-and-white illustrations and some color plates.

Indexes

467. *Art Index.* New York: Wilson, 1929- . Quarterly, with annual cumulations.
This subject index lists periodicals, yearbooks, and museum bulletins on art. It also lists reproductions and indexes current book reviews on art. It is searchable online, through Wilsonline and on CD-ROM from November 1984 on.

468. Art Institute of Chicago. *Index to Art Periodicals.* 11 vols. Boston: G.K. Hall, 1962. 1st supplement, 1975.
This subject index is a photoreproduction of a card index kept by the Ryerson Library of the Art Institute of Chicago. Coverage begins in 1907 and, with the supplement, goes to October 1974.

469. *RILA: International Repertory of the Literature of Art; Repertoire International de la Litterature de l'Art.* Williamstown, Ma.: The Getty Art History Information Program, 1975- . Twice a year.
These volumes index and abstract current publications in Western art history. Coverage is worldwide and on all media. All types of publications are included. Abstracts are descriptive. Organization is chronological, then by type of art. Indexed by author and subject. It is searchable online through DIALOG file 191 from 1973 to the present.

Reproductions

470. *International Directory of Photographic Archives of Works of Art.* 2 vols. Paris: UNESCO, 1954.
These volumes list by country, then by city, then by institution sources for photographs of works of art. Entries list general content of collection, purpose, subjects, availability of negatives, copying services, cataloging, and reproduction rights.

471. Monro, Isabel Stevenson, and Kate M. Monro. *Index to Reproductions of European Paintings: A Guide to Pictures in More than Three Hundred Books.* New York: Wilson, 1956.

This index lists paintings by European artists, including many Victorians. It is a guide to reproductions appearing in 328 books. The main listings are under the names of the artists, with listings under distinctive titles, and some subjects. English-language titles are the preferred form.

472. Havlice, Patricia Pate. *World Painting Index.* 2 vols. Metuchen, N.J.: Scarecrow, 1977. !st supplement, 1973-1980, 1982.

These volumes list reproductions of paintings from artists of all periods and nations. The two original volumes list 1167 books and catalogs published between 1940 and the early part of 1975; the supplement covers 617 books and brings coverage up to 1980. Both the first set and the supplement are arranged in four parts: a numbered bibliography of the books indexed, a listing of works by unknown artists under painting title, a listing by painter, and a listing by painting title with the name of the artist.

Art Libraries

473. Hoffberg, Judith A., and Stanley W. Hess. *Directory of Art Libraries and Visual Resource Collections in North America.* New York: Neal-Schuman, 1978.
This directory is divided into three parts: Part one is a directory of art libraries, part two covers visual resource collections, and part three is an index to these institutions. The United States and Canada are covered. Arrangement is alphabetical by state or province and then by institution. Both library and visual resource sections include information on circulation policy, collections, and services. The art libraries section is indexed by subject categories; the visual resources section is indexed by collection emphasis, by subscription programs available, and by subjects of special collections.

474. Viaux, Jacqueline, comp. *The IFLA Directory of Art Libraries.* New York: Garland, 1985.
This directory lists art libraries from all nations, excluding North America (see item 473). Entries are arranged alphabetically by the official name of the country. Entries are then by city, then by name of institution. Collection size and content given. Subject index. Index of countries.

Catalogs

475. South Kensington Museum, London. National Art
      Library. *Universal Catalogue of Books on Art.* 3
      vols. New York: Burt Franklin, 1870. Reprt.
This listing of books, articles, and transactions covers
books on visual art as of 1870. All European languages are
included. Arrangement is alphabetical by English key word;
A New Collection of Voyages, Discoveries, and Travels and
*Colecion de Estampas de todos los Retratos de los Reyes de
España* are both listed under "Collection." Volume 3 is a
supplement. No indexing.

476. The New York Public Library. *Dictionary Catalog of
      the Art and Architecture Division.* 30 vols.
      Boston: G.K. Hall, 1975.
This catalog lists materials cataloged for the Art and
Architecture Division of the New York Public Library.
Beginning in 1972, all additions to this division are in *The
Dictionary Catalog of the Research Libraries* (New York:
The Library, 1979). In addition, a 1974 supplement
(Boston: G.K. Hall, 1976) lists holdings added from 1972-
1974. Thereafter, an annual, *Bibliographic Guide to Art
and Architecture* (Boston: G.K. Hall, 1976-) lists added
holdings plus material from the Library of Congress MARC
tapes. Together these catalogs provide a uniquely
comprehensive list of publications in the fields of art and
architecture.

Bibliographies

477. The Courtauld Institute of Art. *Bibliography of the History of British Art.* London: Courtauld Institute of Art, v. 1-6, 1934-1946/48; Cambridge: University Press, 1936-56, 6 vols. Title varies.
This subject bibliography of books and articles on British art covers both fine and applied arts. Index in each volume.

Biography

478. Redgrave, Samuel. *A Dictionary of Artists of the English School: Painters, Sculptors, Architects, Engravers, and Ornamentists: With Notices of Their Lives and Works.* London: George Bell and Sons, 1878.
This biographical dictionary lists artists who have worked in England from the Renaissance to the middle of the nineteenth century. Only artists then deceased are included.

479. Strickland, Walter George. *A Dictionary of Irish Artists.* 2 vols. New York: Hacker Art Books, 1968. Reprt 1913 ed.
This dictionary covers Irish artists from earliest times to those deceased by 1912. Biographical entries are lengthy and include a list of the artist's works.

480. Waters, Clara, Erskine Clement, and Lawrence Hutton. *Artists of the Nineteenth Century and Their Works.* New York: Arno Press, 1969.
This biographical dictionary covers Western European artists of the nineteenth century. Brief entries, usually no more than one page, give dates, nationality, chief works, important influences and teachers, and, for some entries, a quotation from a contemporary critic.

Monograms

481. Nahum, Peter. *Monograms of Victorian and Edwardian Artists.* N.p.: Victorian Square Press, 1976.
This book lists the monograms of over 4000 artists, illustrators, craftspeople, and architects working and exhibiting in Great Britain between 1830 and 1930. Arrangement is alphabetical by monogram. Indexed by artist name. A useful one-volume source for information that is otherwise widely scattered.

Philosophy and Psychology

Research Guides

482. DeGeorge, Richard T. *The Philosopher's Guide: To Sources, Research Tools, Professional Life and Related Fields.* Lawrence: The Regents Press of Kansas, 1980.
The guide is a thorough and comprehensive introduction to philosophical research. A scholarly and indispensable tool for anyone seeking information in this field.

483. Douglas, Nancy E., and Nathan Baum. *Library Research Guide to Psychology.* Ann Arbor: Pierian Press, 1983.
This guide is directed at the upper division student beginning to specialize in psychology. The emphasis is on developing an effective search strategy. Computer searching covered.

484. Bynagle, Hans E. *Philosophy: A Guide to the Reference Literature.* Littleton, Co.: Libraries Unlimited, 1986.
This guide to philosophical research will be helpful to anyone starting studies in this field. It is clearly organized, gives information on individual philosophers as well as broader topics, and has several helpful features not included in all such research guides. These include an annotated list of core journals in the field and a listing of principal research centers, professional associations, and other philosophical organizations. It also includes both author/title and subject indexes.

Dictionaries and Encyclopedias

485. Baldwin, James Mark, ed. *Dictionary of Philosophy and Psychology.* 3 vols. New edition with corrections. Gloucester, Ma.: Peter Smith, 1960. Reprt. 1925 ed.
The original edition of this classic dictionary first appeared in 1901. It remains a good source for nineteenth-century perceptions of philosophy and psychology, though American in its bias.

486. Edwards, Paul, ed. *The Encyclopedia of Philosophy.* New York: Macmillan; London: Collier-Macmillan, 1967.
This classic encyclopedia is still the first source for identification and summary of the work of philosophers, descriptions of philosophical schools, and definitions of philosophical terms. Articles are signed and include excellent bibliographies of both primary and secondary works.

487. Lacey, A.R. *A Dictionary of Philosophy.* London: Routledge & Kegan Paul, 1976.
This one-volume dictionary of philosophy is aimed at the layman or beginning student. Its emphasis is on explaining terminology, with a lesser emphasis on individual philosophers. Longer and more important entries include a brief bibliography.

488. Corsini, Raymond J., ed. *Encyclopedia of Psychology.* 4 vols. New York: John Wiley and Sons, 1984.
This encyclopedia provides useful definitions of psychological terms, biographies of important figures, and essays on the history of various psychological fields. Articles are signed.

Indexes and Abstracts

489. *International Political Science Abstracts.*
     Documentation politique internationale. Oxford:
     Blackwell, 1951- . Quarterly. Publisher
     varies.
This abstract lists and summarizes periodical articles
published in many countries and languages. The section on
"Political Thinkers and Ideas" lists articles of interest to
Victorian scholars. Abstracts are in English or French.

490. *Philosopher's Index: An International Index to*
     Philosophical Periodicals and Books. Bowling
     Green, Ohio: Bowling Green State University
     Press, 1967- . Quarterly with annual
     cumulations. Title varies.
Arrangement and coverage varies. Current volumes cover
books and periodicals, and non-English language material
is included. Arrangement is alphabetical by subject, with a
separate author index. All aspects of philosophy and
philosophers of all periods are covered. Includes abstracts.
A retrospective edition, *The Philosopher's Index: A*
Retrospective Index to U. S. Publications From 1940
(Bowling Green, Ohio: Bowling Green State University
Press, 1978) extends coverage to the period 1940-1976.
Available as DIALOG file 57 back to 1940.

491. *Psychological Abstracts.* Lancaster, Pa.: American
     Psychological Association, 1927- . Monthly.
     Place of publication varies.
This abstract covers books, articles, reports, and
scientific documents in psychology. Arrangement is by
classification, with author index and, beginning in 1963,
brief subject index. Cumulated author and subject indexes
come out quarterly and annually. Aiding subject searching
is the *Cumulative Subject Index to "Psychological*
Abstracts" (Boston: G.K. Hall, 1966). Available as DIALOG
file 11 from 1967 to the present and as BRS file PSYC.

Bibliographies

492. Rand, Benjamin, comp. *Bibliography of Philosophy,*
      Psychology, and Cognate Subjects. 2 parts. Vol.
      3 J.M. Baldwin. *Dictionary of Philosophy and*
      Psychology. Gloucester, Mass.: Peter Smith,
      1960. Reprt. Macmillan, 1905.
This dictionary and bibliography are guides to Victorian
publications on philosophy and psychology. The dictionary
gives short entries on persons and longer articles on major
issues in philosophy. The bibliography is in two sections,
the first by personal names, the second by topic.

493. Guerry, Herbert, ed. and comp. *A Bibliography of*
      Philosophical Bibliographies. Westport, Conn.:
      Greenwood Press, 1977.
This bibliography has set itself the task of collecting
"philosophical bibliographies published in all countries
since 1450 ... through the year 1974." The bibliographies
listed appeared, for the most part, as separate publications
or in journals. A few exceptions first appeared as
appendixes to monographs. The book is arranged in two
sections, the first covering individual philosophers and the
second philosophical topics. Author index.

Dissertations

494. Bechtle, Thomas C., and Mary F. Riley.
      Dissertations in Philosophy Accepted at
      American Universities, 1861-1975. New
      York: Garland, 1978.
This bibliography lists dissertations in philosophy
from120 universities in the United States and Canada. It is
accurate and lists materials from earlier periods than are
available in most annual lists. Organization is alphabetic
by names and topics such as "aesthetics" and "language."

Photography

Research Guides

495. Sennett, Robert S. *The Nineteenth-Century Photographic Press: A Study Guide.* New York: Garland, 1987.
This guide lists photographic material published in journals in Europe and American between 1840 and 1900. The bibliography is arranged alphabetically by the title of the journal. Entries give dates, some give the editor and noteworthy facts about the journal. The more important journals have a partial list of contents giving notable articles. Indexed by subject and personal name.

496. Edwards, Gary. *International Guide to Nineteenth-Century Photographers and Their Works.* Boston: G.K. Hall, 1988.
This guide lists over 4,000 photographers of the nineteenth century. Arrangement is alphabetical and entries include information on nationality, dates, subject matter, dates for earliest and last known photos, processes and formats used, studio location, geographic settings when appropriate, and locations for sales. Also included is an index to catalogs from 51 dealers or auction houses. This is an extremely useful source on often fugitive material.

Bibliographies

497. Boni, Albert, ed. *Photographic Literature.* New York: Morgan & Morgan, 1962. *Photographic Literature, 1960-1970.* Hastings-on-Hudson, NY: Morgan & Morgan, 1972.
These volumes list periodical and book publications on all aspects of photography. Arrangement is by subject. No annotations, but a symbol by some entries designates recommended works. Indexed by author.

498. Barger, M. Susan, comp. *Bibliography of Photographic Processes in Use Before 1880: Their Materials, Processing, and Conservation.* Rochester, NY: Graphic Arts Research Center, 1980.
This bibliography covers all aspects of the care and preservation of mid-nineteenth century photographs. It lists photographic journals and manuals of the pre-1880 period. Entries are arranged topically and have brief annotations. Author and keyword indexes. Useful source for much otherwise unindexed material.

499. Gernsheim, Helmut. *Incunabula of British Photographic Literature: A Bibliography of British Photographic Literature 1839-75 and British Books Illustrated with Original Photographs.* London: Scolar Press, 1984.
This bibliography lists British books illustrated with original photographs, as opposed to those having photographs reproduced. Part II covers the literature of photography, 1839-1875. Part III lists journals and important essays on photography. Entries are annotated. Indexed by photographers and a general index.

Indexes

500. *International Photography Index.* Boston: G.K. Hall,
     1979-1984.
     Index to Articles on Photography. Rochester: Visual
     Studies Workshop Press, 1977-78.
These indexes cover articles on photography "as a medium
of creative expression, or a vehicle for communication, or
that deal with the history of photography and its
practitioners." Despite the title and publisher change, the
second volume is a continuation of the first.

Religion

Research Guides

501. Purvis, J.S. *An Introduction to Ecclesiastical Records.* London: St. Anthony's Press, 1953.
This book is intended as an elementary introduction to the use and interpretation of ecclesiastical records. The guide is divided into three parts: Chapter One, Definitions and Archbishops' Registers; Chapter Two, The Records of Visitation; and Chapter Three, Ecclesiastical Courts. Each chapter is divided into sections by the different types of records within that category.

502. Kennedy, James R., Jr. *Library Research Guide to Religion and Theology.* 2nd ed., revised. Ann Arbor: Pierian Press, 1984.
This is an excellent guide to using the library for research in religion and theology. Aimed at the upper division undergraduate or the beginning graduate student, it addresses the problem of evaluating sources, as well as giving the usual list of reference books. Basic and helpful.

503. The Royal Commission on Historical Manuscripts. *Papers of British Churchmen, 1780-1940.* Guides to Sources for British History. London: HMSO, 1987.
"This guide describes the papers of over 800 churchmen and women active during the period 1780-1940, selected on the basis of their significance for the study of British ecclesiastical history." As with the other volumes in this series, the papers listed here are those in the possession of the individual at the time of his or her death. Various Christian denominations are included.

Dictionaries and Encyclopedias

504. Hastings, James, ed. *Encyclopedia of Religion and Ethics.* 13 vols. New York: Scribners, 1908.
This classic encyclopedia of religion and ethics is useful both for the information it conveys in long, well-researched articles and for nineteenth-century religious views. Articles cover a wide range of topics, both non-Christian and Christian, are signed, and include bibliographies.

505. Ollard, S.L., ed., assisted by Gordon Crosse. *Dictionary of English Church History.* London: A.R. Mowbray, 1912.
This dictionary covers people, places, events, and terms of importance in English Church history. It covers the English church only, omitting other British churches.

506. Purvis, J.S. *Dictionary of Ecclesiastical Terms.* London: Thomas Nelson and sons, 1962.
This dictionary is a guide to ecclesiastical language for the nonspecialist. The point of view is High Church.

507. Farmer, David Hugh. *The Oxford Dictionary of Saints.* Oxford: Clarendon Press, 1978.
This volume is a selective list of saints, including all English saints, all saints having a sizable cult in England, the most important and representative saints of Ireland, Scotland, and Wales, non-British or Irish saints of importance in Church history, and Byzantine saints.

508.   *New Catholic Encyclopedia.* Prepared by an editorial
       staff at The Catholic University of America. 17
       vols. New York: McGraw-Hill, 1967-1981.
       Reprt. Palatine, Ill.: Publishers Guide, 1981.
This is an excellent encyclopedia with a Catholic viewpoint.
It covers secular subjects, but its real strengths are
theology and religious history. Volumes 16 and 17 update
information on the Church since Vatican Council II.

509.   Cross, F.L., and E.A. Livingstone, eds. *Oxford
       Dictionary of the Christian Church.* 2nd ed.
       Oxford: Oxford University Press, 1983.
This dictionary covers all aspects of organized religion,
with special emphasis on English churches. Articles are
short but thorough, with a bibliography at the end of most.

510.   Eliade, Mircea, ed. in chief. *The Encyclopedia of
       Religion.* 16 vols. New York: Macmillan, 1987-
       88.
This excellent work, covering all religions and all aspects
of religion, incorporates the most recent scholarly
methodologies. Articles are signed and include useful basic
bibliographies. The index is thorough and an important
guide to the complex subjects covered in the longer
articles. For example, information on the Oxford Movement
is found in biographical articles on its major figures, but
no single article appears under that phrase.

Yearbooks

511. Church of England. *Yearbook.* London: Church Information Office and Society for Promoting Christian Knowledge, 1882- . Title varies: 1883-1962, Church of England. National Assembly. *Official Yearbook.*

This yearbook gives general directory information on the Church of England, plus biographical information on members of the General Synod, bishops, deans, provosts, archdeacons, and Lambeth Palace staff.

Indexes

512. Richardson, Ernest Cushing, comp. and ed. *Periodical Articles on Religion; An Alphabetical Subject Index and Index Encyclopedia to Periodical Articles on Religion, 1890-1899.* New York: Published for the Hartford Seminary Press by Charles Scribner's Sons, 1911. Also *Author Index.*

These indexes cover religious articles, usually from periodicals devoted to religion, published between 1890-1899. The main volume is organized by subject. The author volume is alphabetical by name, with unsigned articles under the first word of the title. Periodicals in major European languages are covered, with many American titles.

513. *Catholic Periodical and Literature Index.* v. 14- ,
      1967/68.   Bimonthly,   with   biennial
      cumulations.
This index combines *Catholic Periodical Index* (1939-67)
and *The Guide to Catholic Literature* (1888-1967). It
indexes a selected list of Catholic periodicals, gives
subject, author, and title listings for adult books by
Catholics, and lists a selection of books of interest to
Catholics by non-Catholic authors. All of the indexes
emphasized American authors.

514. *Religion Index One: Periodicals. Religion Index Two:
      Multi-Author   Works.*   Chicago: American
      Theological Seminary, 1977- . Continues *Index
      to Religious Periodical Literature.* 1949-76.
These publications index periodicals, festschriften, and
other multi-author works. Indexes appear yearly, with
cumulations issued periodically, most recently every two
years. Each volume contains three indexes: A subject index,
with complete citation; an author index, with an abstract of
the article; and a book review section, listed by the author
of the reviewed book. These indexes are good sources for
English church history. They also include studies on
religion in art, literature, psychology, and other subjects.
They can be searched online, through Wilsonline, DIALOG
file 190, BRS file RELI, and on a CD-ROM based on the
Wilson index. The indexes are integrated in these
electronic formats. The Wilsonline database and CD-ROM
go back to 1975; DIALOG and BRS go back to 1975 for
periodicals and 1960 for multiauthor works. The databases
are updated three times weekly.

Bibliographies

515. Case, S.J., and others. *A Bibliographical Guide to the History of Christianity.* Chicago: University of Chicago Press, 1931.
This selective bibliography covers the history of Christianity. Chapter VI covers the British Isles. Emphasis is on earlier periods of Christianity (pre-1689), but some items deal with Victorian topics.

516. MacGregor, Malcolm B. *The Sources and Literature of Scottish Church History.* Glasgow: John McCallum, 1934.
This bibliography lists the literature of Scottish church history. Organization is by type of material and then by period or by more specific subject. Entries may have brief annotations. Subject index.

517. Barrow, John G. *A Bibliography of Bibliographies in Religion.* Ann Arbor: Edwards Brothers, 1955.
This is a useful and thorough list of bibliographies on all aspects of religion and religious history. Topically arranged, good indexing helps with access.

518. Chadwick, Owen. *The History of the Church: A Select Bibliography.* Helps for Students of History. London: The Historical Association, 1962.
This brief guide to the history of the Christian church in Europe includes a short section on the English Church in the nineteenth century and after. Citations are briefly and usefully annotated.

519. Walsh, Michael J., and others, comps. *Religious Bibliographies in Serial Literature: A Guide.* London: Mansell, 1981.

This bibliography lists bibliographies of religious studies appearing in serial literature of all fields. Arrangement is alphabetical by source. Entries include title, subtitle, bibliographic information, publishing history, layout of publication, material covered by the bibliography, an evaluative comment, publisher's name and address, and ISSN. A modest, thorough, and useful guide.

520. Eisen, Sydney, and Bernard V. Lightman. *Victorian Science and Religion: A Bibliography with Emphasis on Evolution, Belief, and Unbelief, Comprised of Works Published from c. 1900-1975.* Hamden, Conn.: Archon, 1984.

This bibliography lists a wide range of materials, including books, articles, and dissertations on the connection and conflict between science and religion during the Victorian period. It covers writings about the period 1830 to 1900. The three sections are: A) Main Currents; B) Natural Theology, Geology, and Evolution; and C) Religion— Ideas and Institutions. These section are divided by subject categories. Author and subject indexes.

521. Menendez, Albert J. *The Road to Rome.* New York: Garland, 1986.

Most of the books listed here are nineteenth and twentieth century conversion narratives. The sections are: Personal Testimonies; Autobiographies of Converts; Biographies of Converts; Methods and Techniques of Conversion; and Novels of Conversion. Author index. Entries not annotated.

522. Crumb, Lawrence N. *The Oxford Movement and Its
       Leaders: A Bibliography of Secondary and Lesser
       Primary Sources.* ATLA Bibliography Series.
       No. 24. Metuchen, N.J.: The American
       Theological Library Association and The
       Scarecrow Press, 1988.
This bibliography lists in chronological order the
literature by and about the Oxford Movement. The list
begins with 1829 and goes through 1987. Author,
periodical, and subject indexes. Entries for scholarly
books include a list of reviews.

523. Moyles, R.G. *A Bibliography of Salvation Army
       Literature in English (1865-1987).* Texts and
       Studies in Religion. Queenston, Ontario: Edwin
       Mellen, 1988.
This bibliography traces the literature by and about the
Salvation Army from its beginnings in 1865 as The East
London Christian Mission. Arrangement is topical.
Manuscript material in the various Salvation Army
archives is not included. Author index. Good source for
much fugitive material.

Biography

524. *Crockford's Clerical Directory.* Oxford: Oxford
       University Press, 1858- . Frequency varies.
This directory gives biographical sketches of Church of
England clergy and statistical information on the Church.

525. Baring-Gould, S., and John Fisher. *The Lives of the British Saints: The Saints of Wales and Cornwall and Such Irish Saints as Have Dedications in Britain.* 4 vols. London: Published for the Honourable Society of Cymmrodorion by Charles J. Clark, 1907.

This illustrated biographical dictionary gives essays on the lives of the saints of England, Scotland, Wales, and of some Irish saints. The introductory material in the first volume discusses several topics relating to the Welsh and Cornish saints. Volume 4 contains an index for the set.

526. Delaney, John J., and James Edward Tobin. *Dictionary of Catholic Biography.* Garden City, N.Y.: Doubleday, 1961.

This dictionary gives short biographical sketches and suggestions for further readings on important Roman Catholics from all nations and times. Nineteenth-century English Catholics, including important converts, are well covered.

527. Moyer, Elgin S. *Who was Who in Church History.* Chicago: Moody Press, 1962.

Church history is broadly defined in this biographical dictionary. Both Protestants and Catholics are included, as well as noted atheists and enemies of Christianity. Many notable Victorians are included.

History of Science and Technology

Dictionaries

528. Bynum, W.F., E.J. Browne, and Roy Porter, eds. *Dictionary of the History of Science.* Princeton, N.J.: Princeton University Press, 1981.
This dictionary gives concise explanations of words and concepts commonly used in the history of science. Articles are signed with initials of authors and short bibliographies follow longer articles. A biographical index identifies the nationality of the scientist and lists articles in which that name appears.

529. *McGraw-Hill Encyclopedia of Science and Technology.* 6th ed. 20 vols. New York: McGraw-Hill, 1987.
This encyclopedia is the standard resource for overviews of scientific topics. Emphasis is on current scientific information, but plentiful historical information is also included, both as background in topical articles and under the names of leading scientists. Bibliographies.

Chronology

530. Parkinson, Claire L. *Breakthroughs: A Chronology of Great Achievements in Science and Mathematics.* Boston: G.K. Hall, 1985.
This chronology lists the major achievements each year in science from 1200 to 1930. Within each year are listed the name of the science, with a paragraph on that year's events. In addition to the chronology, a list of sources, and a name and a subject index are included.

531. Gascoigne, Robert Mortimer. *A Chronology of the History of Science, 1450-1900.* New York: Garland, 1987.
This chronology extends from 1472 to the 1890s and covers eighteen science categories and most European countries. Part 1 is arranged by subject; Part 2 by countries or regions. Indexed by persons and institutions.

Indexes

532. Royal Society of London. *Catalogue of Scientific Papers, 1800-1900.* 19 vols. London: Clay, 1867-1902; Cambridge: University Press, 1914-1925.
This catalog was compiled as an index to scientific papers in "the Transactions of Societies, Journals, and other Periodical works." Arrangement is by author's name in the two main volumes. Seventeen volumes of index, one for each of the classifications in the Schedules of the International Catalogue, provide a very general subject approach to the material. A subject index to the earlier volumes (Cambridge: Cambridge University Press, 1908) increases their usefulness. An excellent source for many otherwise lost documents of Victorian science.

533. *Current Technology Index.* London: Library Association, 1981- .
This index is the continuation of *British Technology Index* (London: Library Association, 1962-80). An index to British technological journals, it includes articles on the history of technology. Listings are under subject (Railways), with subheadings for historical articles (Railways: Great Britain—History).

Catalogs

534.   Clark, Alan J. *Book Catalogue of the Library of the Royal Society.* 5 vols. N.p.: University Publication of America, 1982.

The Royal Society, founded in 1660, is the oldest continually existing national scientific academy in the world. A library was started early in its existence and now holds over 4500 titles. This set is a recataloging of the collection up to November 30, 1981. Entries are arranged alphabetically, word by word, under individual or corporate authors. Bibliographic data is in general accordance with the 1967 *Anglo-American Cataloging Rules.*

535.   Gascoigne, Robert Mortimer. *A Historical Catalogue of Scientists and Scientific Books From the Earliest Times to the Close of the Nineteenth Century.* New York: Garland, 1984.

This catalog is both a biographical dictionary and a list of significant scientific books. Coverage is to the close of the nineteenth century. Section three covers the eighteenth and nineteenth centuries and is divided by science. Within the sciences, arrangement is chronological. The volume is useful for its overview of important names in science, but it would be stronger with some indexing.

536.   Gascoigne, Robert Mortimer. *A Historical Catalogue of Scientific Periodicals, 1665-1900, With a Survey of Their Development.* New York: Garland, 1985.

The first part of this catalog lists about 900 scientific periodicals published from 1665 to 1900. Arrangement is by science and then chonological. Part 2 covers "Selection of the Periodicals and Their Relative Sizes," with a chapter devoted to the nineteenth century. Part 3 discusses "The Development of the Periodical Literature." Indexed by titles, personal names, institutions and cities.

General Science and Technology

537. Whitrow, Magda, ed. *ISIS Cumulative Bibliography: A Bibliography of Science Formed from ISIS Critical Bibliographies 1-90, 1913-65.* 3 vols. London: Mansell, 1971.
Neu, John, ed. *ISIS Cumulative Bibliography, 1966-1975.* London: Mansell, 1980.
Isis: Cumulative Index, Volumes 44-73, 1953-1982. Philadelphia: Department of History and Sociology of Science, University of Pennsylvania, 1985.

These volumes index the *Isis Critical Bibliography.* This bibliography is central to the study of the history of science, appearing since the journal *Isis* began in 1913 and listing publications on the history of science.

538. *Scientific Research in British Universities and Colleges.* London: HMSO, 1951/52- . Annual. Title and frequency vary.

This annual is arranged by broad subject, with a section for each science on "History and Philosophy of Science." Arrangement within subject section is by university. It also includes non-academic research institutes and projects of PhD candidates. Name and subject indexes.

539. Sarton George. *A Guide to the History of Science: A First Guide for the Study of the History of Science With Introductory Essays on Science and Tradition.* New York: Ronald Press, 1952.

Though the citations in this volume are dated, as an introduction to techniques and to older sources on the history of science it is still basic. The first part consists of three lectures on the purpose and meaning of the history of science; the second is a bibliographic guide to the subject. Useful to the Victorianist are the sections on "History of Science in Special Countries" and on "Institutes, Museums, Libraries." Index of proper names.

540.   Ferguson, Eugene S. *A Bibliography of the History of Technology.* Cambridge, Mass.: The Society for the History of Technology and The M.I.T. Press, 1968.
This bibliography lists and evaluates both primary and secondary literature in the history of technology. Emphasis is on the U.S., but other countries, including Great Britain are well covered. Excellent annotations. Indexed.

541.   Rider, K.J. *The History of Science and Technology: A Select Bibliography for Students.* 2nd ed. London: The Library Association, 1970.
This bibliography treats in two sections the histories of science and of technology. Though badly outdated, it is well organized and still useful for basic titles.

542.   Durbin, Paul T. *A Guide to the Culture of Science, Technology, and Medicine.* New York: The Free Press, 1980.
This guide discusses the state of the field in nine areas dealing with science, technology, and medicine. The areas are: history of science, history of technology, history of medicine, philosophy of science, philosophy of technology, philosophy of medicine, sociology of science and technology in medicine, and science policy studies. Chapters include discussions of the history of the discipline, current concerns in the field, research methodologies, and a basic bibliography, plus material and concerns unique to each field. Helpful analytical table of contents and good index. Excellent source for those approaching the fields for the first time.

543.   Jayawardene, S.A., comp. *Reference Books for the
       Historian of Science.* London: Science Museum,
       1982.
This handlist covers both general and specialized reference
materials. Part I covers the history and literature of
science; Part II covers general history; and Part III
contains general reference materials. Excellent indexes by
author/title and by subject. No annotations.

544.   Hurt, C.D. *Information Sources in Science and
       Technology.* Englewood, Co.: Libraries
       Unlimited, 1988.
The first section of this guide is devoted to sources on the
history of science. Division within the section is by
specific science. Citations are briefly annotated.
Annotations are descriptive. The intended audience is
librarians interested in building collections, but the book
would be of use to anyone starting research in this area.

Astronomy

545.   DeVorkin, David H. *The History of Modern
       Astronomy and Astrophysics: A Selected,
       Annotated Bibliography.* Bibliographies of the
       History of Science and Technology, Vol. 1. New
       York: Garland, 1982.
This bibliography covers the history of astronomy and
astrophysics starting with the eighteenth century.
Organization is topical, with only the section on "Textbooks
and Popular Works" divided by century. Annotations
describe the contents of the article or book. Subject and
author index.

Biochemistry

546. Fruton, Joseph S. *A Bio-Bibliography for the History of the Biochemical Sciences Since 1800.* Philadelphia: American Philosophical Society, 1982.

This bibliography provides information on biographical and bibliographical books and articles on those in the biochemical sciences. Arrangement is alphabetical by name. Entries include no annotations.

Biology and Natural History

547. Bottle, R.T., and H.V. Wyatt, ed. *The Use of Biological Literature.* Hamden, Conn.: Archon Books, 1971.

This guide to research, though dated in many ways, is useful to historians of science for its chapter on "History and Biography of Biology," by J.L. Thornton and R.I.J. Tully.

548. Smit, Pieter. *History of the Life Sciences: An Annotated Bibliography.* New York: Hafner, 1974.

This bibliography is nearly exhaustive and has annotations of unusual clarity and usefulness. However, its organization makes it difficult to use for research on a particular time or place. The time divisions for modern Europe are large; the Victorian period is covered in the section "Renaissance and Later." Subdivisions are by science. Personal name index only.

549. Freeman, Richard Broke. *British Natural History
        Books, 1495-1900: A Handlist.* Hamden, Conn.:
        Archon Books, 1980.
This handlist of books on natural history is in two parts,
the first alphabetical, the second chronological. Full
citations are given in the first section, brief author-title
listings in the second. The introduction defines "natural
history" and discusses the scope of the list. Subject index.

550. Overmier, Judith A. *The History of Biology: A
        Selected Annotated Bibliography.* Bibliographies
        of the History of Science and Technology. New
        York: Garland, 1989.
This bibliography of secondary sources covers biology
from the eighteenth century to the mid-twentieth century.
It is selective. Criteria include quality and
representativeness. Selected foreign-language works are
included, but most entries are in English. Annotations are
descriptive. Author index. Introductory level.

Chemistry and Chemical
Technology

551. Smith, Henry Monmouth. *Torchbearers of
        Chemistry: Portraits and Brief Biographies of
        Scientists Who have Contributed to the Making
        of Modern Chemistry.* New York: Academic
        Press, 1949.
This book gives portraits and brief identifications of
important chemists from the Middle Ages to the twentieth
century in alphabetical order. The bibliography of
bibliographies is also arranged alphabetically by the name
of the subject.

552. Multhauf, Robert P. *The History of Chemical Technology: An Annotated Bibliography.* New York: Garland, 1984.
This bibliography on sources for the history of chemical technology contains much helpful and otherwise difficult-to-obtain information for the historian of science. Part I includes a section on national histories, including that of Great Britain. The second and third sections cover specific substances. Author and title indexes.

Data Processing

553. Cortada, James W. *An Annotated Bibliography on the History of Data Processing.* Westport, Conn.: Greenwood, 1983.
This annotated bibliography is not an obvious source for the scholar of Victorian studies. However, the coverage is thorough enough to include Babbage and other early developers of the theory behind data processing. The second section, "From Punched Cards to Digital Computers, 1800-1939," contains this material. Author index. No geographical approach.

Earth Sciences

554. Matthews, Edward B. "Catalogue of Published Bibliographies in Geology, 1896-1920." *Bulletin of the National Research Council* 6 (Oct. 1923).
Arranged alphabetically by topic, this catalog is a good start in establishing the parameters of Victorian knowledge of geology.

555. Porter, Roy. *The Earth Sciences: An Annotated Bibliography.* Bibliographies of the History of Science and Technology, Vol. 3. New York: Garland, 1983.
This selective bibliography covers all aspects of geological science, including social causes and consequences of geological discoveries. The organization provides several approaches to the subject: by branch of the science, by geographical area, and by special subjects. Subject and personal name index. Entries are annotated.

556. Brush, Stephen G., and Helmut E. Landsberg. *The History of Geophysics and Meteorology: An Annotated Bibliography.* Bibliographies of the History of Science and Technology, Vol. 7. New York: Garland, 1985.
This bibliography includes information on the history of the study of the physics of the earth, the origin and development of the solar system, and the formation of the earth's surface. Coverage begins with early, classic works, though emphasis is on the twentieth century. Organization is topical. Name index and subject index. Organization makes it difficult to search by period.

Electronics

557. Shiers, George, and May Shiers. *Bibliography of the History of Electronics.* Metuchen, N.J.: Scarecrow, 1972.
This annotated bibliography lists books, articles, reports, and other printed materials on the history of electronics and telecommunications from about 1860 to recent times. Arrangement is mainly topical, though the opening chapters deal with general reference works, serials, general histories, and biographies. Author and subject indexes. Annotations are descriptive, with some comments on level or importance of work. Only works in English are listed. No access by period or date.

558. Davis, Henry B. *Electrical and Electronic Technologies: A Chronology of Events and Inventors to 1900.* Metuchen, N.J.: Scarecrow, 1981.
This chronology of the history of electrical and electronic technologies devotes over half the entries to the nineteenth century. The book is more than a simple chronology, as a descriptive biographical note is appended to each listing. Subject index.

Engineering

559. Stapleton, Darwin H. *The History of Civil Engineering Since 1600: An Annotated Bibliography.* Bibliographies of the History of Science and Technology, Vol. 4. New York: Garland, 1986.
This bibliography covers material through early 1985. Entries are arranged first chronologically, with a section devoted to 1830-1900, and then by topic. Most entries are for secondary sources and have brief annotations. Various languages are included. Author and name index.

Mathematics

560. Pemberton, John E. *How to Find Out in Mathematics: A Guide to Sources of Information.* 2nd revised ed. Oxford, Pergamon Press, 1969.
Despite its age, this is still the most comprehensive guide to finding information on all aspects of mathematics. Chapter 8, "Mathematical History and Biography," covers material of interest to Victorianists.

561. May, Kenneth Ownsworth. *Bibliography and*
      Research Manual of the History of Mathematics.
      Toronto: University of Toronto Press, 1973.
This bibliography lists about 31,000 entries of secondary
literature on the history of mathematics. Its great strength
is the number of access points. Material can be searched by
time period or by country. No annotations.

562. Dauben, Joseph Warren. *The History of*
      Mathematics From Antiquity to the Present: A
      Selective Bibliography. New York: Garland,
      1985.
This bibliography covers the history of mathematics,
including a section on "Mathematics in the 19th Century."
The section is divided into subsections: "Bibliographies,"
Source Books and Surveys," "Journals," "General
Histories," "Biographical Studies," "Special Studies,"
"Foundations," and "Institutions." Entries are annotated.
The subject index is largely personal names and is not
useful in restricting geographical area.

Mining

563. Molloy, Peter M. *The History of Metal Mining and*
      Metallurgy: An Annotated Bibliography. New
      York: Garland, 1986.
This bibliography of secondary works covers mining and
mining technology throughout history and worldwide.
Social, economic, and technical history are included.
Arrangement is topical and entries are briefly annotated.

Physics

564. Yates, B. *How to Find Out About Physics: A Guide to Sources of Information Arranged by the Decimal Classification.* Oxford: Pergamon Press, 1965.
This guide to reference sources in physics includes a section on biographical and historical reference books. Though much work has been done in the history of science since this guide first appeared, it is still useful for classics in the field. Emphasis is on British publications.

565. Bush, Stephen, and Lanfranco Belloni. *The History of Modern Physics: An International Bibliography.* Bibliographies of the History of Science and Technology, Vol. 4. New York: Garland 1983.
"Modern physics" is defined in this book as "physics since the discovery of x-rays in 1895"; therefore emphasis is not on the Victorian period. However some information on late nineteenth century science is to be found here. The organization and annotations assume familiarity with the general field of physics and the history of science. Annotations are brief and descriptive. Name, subject, and institutional indexes.

566. Home, R.W. *The History of Classical Physics: A Selected, Annotated Bibliography.* Bibliographies of the History of Science and Technology, Vol. 8. New York: Garland, 1984.
This bibliography covers the period 1700 to 1900. Its emphasis is on current historical writing rather than primary sources. Organized first by period than by topics within physics, the organization lends itself to focus on a particular period. Entires are annotated for central argument of work. Personal name index.

Biography

567. Ireland, Norma Olin. *Index to Scientists of the World from Ancient to Modern Times: Biographies and Portraits.* Boston, Mass.: Faxon, 1962.
This volume indexes collected biographies of scientists from all periods, nations, and sciences.

568. Gillispie, Charles Coulston, ed. *Dictionary of Scientific Biography.* 16 vols. New York: Scribner's, 1970-80.
This biographical dictionary has extensive signed articles on major scientific figures from all countries and periods. The articles include not only biographical facts but also evaluation of the subject's contribution to scientific knowledge. A lengthy bibliography follows each entry. The fifteenth volume is a supplement containing brief biographies and topical essays; volume 16 is an index.

569. *Archives of British Men of Science.* London: Mansell Information, 1972. 64 microfiche.
This directory on microfiche covers British men and women scientists active 1870-1950, giving information on the existence, character, and location of their correspondence, personal papers, and unpublished writings. The guide produced by Roy M. MacLeod and James R. Friday, *Archives of British Men of Science* (London: Mansell, 1972), gives the scientists listed with microfiche numbers and frame. The guide also discusses the method by which the information was gained.

570. The Royal Commission on Historical Manuscripts. *The Manuscript Papers of British Scientists, 1600-1940.* Guides to Sources for British History. London: HMSO, 1982.
This guide gives descriptions and locations for the manuscript papers of 635 British scientists, many of them active during the nineteenth century.

571. Williams, Trevor I., ed. *A Biographical Dictionary of Scientists.* 3rd ed. London: Adam & Charles Balck, 1982.
This biographical dictionary covers deceased scientists from all fields and nations, with good coverage of British scientists. The short biographies include evaluation of the scientist's contribution to science and further sources of information.

572. Herzenberg, Caroline L. *Women Scientists from Antiquity to the Present: An Index.* West Cornwall, CT.: Locust Hill Press, 1986.
This index lists about 2500 women from 130 works on scientists. Entries give name, field, dates, nationality, and list of sources. Indexed by field. Emphasis is on the U.S., but British women are well covered.

Sociology and Anthropology

573. *International Bibliography of Sociology/*
     Bibliographie Internationale de sociologie.
     London: Tavistock; Chicago: Aldine, 1952- .
     Annual. Publisher and title vary.
This annual bibliography includes a section on the historical development of sociology. It covers all languages and nations. Indexes by author and subject.

574. *Sociological Abstracts.* New York: Sociological
     Abstracts, 1952- . Frequency varies. Now
     published 6 times a year, with the last issue a
     cumulative index for the year.
This abstract lists a broad range of sociological articles in periodicals. The subject index includes the heading "Nineteenth Century" and articles of interest to the Victorianists may be found here. Searchable as DIALOG file 37 and on BRS file SOCA.

575. Kemper, Robert V., and John F.S. Phinney. *The*
     History of Anthropology: A Research Guide. New
     York: Garland, 1977.
This bibliography is divided into five sections: General Sources; Background; Modern Anthropology; Related Social Sciences; and Bibliographical Sources. Most of the material of interest to the Victorianist comes in the Background section. Listings with sections are by broad topic. Author index.

576. Bart, Pauline, and Linda Frankel. *The Student Sociologist's Handbook.* 4th ed. New York: Random House, 1986.
This guide is directed to the student beginning to write papers in the field of sociology. It covers a wide range of subjects of concern to such a student, including techniques and formats in writing a paper, mechanics of research in a library, major periodicals, and specific research materials. The emphasis is on sociology as the study of current society, but some mention is made of periodicals on history and society and some reference tools on this subject. A final chapter on the computer and sociology covers word processing and computational needs but does not address online data bases and other information sources.

Theater and Drama

Research Guides

577. Whalon, Marion K. *Performing Arts Research: A Guide to Information Sources.* Performing Arts Information Guide Series. Detroit: Gale, 1976.
This guide to research covers sources useful for all aspects of theater and performing arts research. Organization is by type of source. Indexed by author, title, and subject. Good source for students unfamiliar with research in this field.

578. Bailey, Claudia Jean. *A Guide to Reference and Bibliography for Theatre Research.* 2nd ed. Columbus, Ohio: The Ohio State University Libraries Publications Committee, 1983.
This guide to research in theater begins with general reference sources useful to those doing research in this area. The second section deals with sources specifically on theater and drama. Bibliographic citations include brief annotations. Author/title index.

Surveys and Dictionaries

579. Hartnoll, Phyllis, ed. *The Oxford Companion to the Theatre.* 4th ed. Oxford: Oxford University Press, 1983.
This book is a typical "Oxford Companion" in arrangement and approach. Names and terms are arranged alphabetically and identified in short essays. Longer essays on the theater in particular nations are included and excellent, lengthy articles on technical matters.

580. Banham, Martin, ed. *The Cambridge Guide to World Theatre.* Cambridge: Cambridge University Press, 1988.
The Cambridge guides are similar to those produced by Oxford. Brief articles and identifications are give for all aspects of the theater. Especially good on British theater.

Bibliographies

Though I have largely excluded subject histories from this guide, the two following entries are histories of English drama. They are included because of the important bibliographies in them. Both are such central works, as both histories and bibliographies, that it is difficult to imagine doing research on English drama without their aid.

581. Nicoll, Allardyce. *A History of English Drama, 1660-1900.* Cambridge: The University Press. Vol. IV, 1800-1850, 1955. Vol. V, 1850-1900, 1959. Vol. VI, A Short-Title Alphabetical Catalogue of Plays, 1965.
This work provides both an important overview of the history of English drama and invaluable bibliographic information. Volumes IV and V include essays on the theater and a handlist of plays arranged alphabetically by author. Volume VI serves as an index to the complete set and gives title access to the material in the handlists.

582. Arnott, J.F., and J.W. Robinson. *English Theatrical Literature, 1559-1900: A Bibliography Incorporating Robert W. Lowe's "A Bibliographical Account of English Theatrical Literature" Published in 1888.* London: Society for Theatre Research, 1970.
This annotated listing of theatrical literature covers works on the theater, as opposed to drama, published between 1559 and 1900. Arrangement is chronological within classified sections. Only separately published works are listed. Indexed by author, title, and place of publication, it is difficult to search by subject due to the lack of a subject index. The bibliography is an update of item 584.

583. Craik, T.W., ed. *The Revels History of Drama in English.* London: Methuen. Vol. VI, 1750-1880, 1975. Vol. VII, 1880 to the present, 1978.
These two volumes cover major plays of the Victorian theater, with descriptions of the plots of the plays and of their peformances. Important bibliographic essays are included in both volumes.

584. Lowe, Robert W. *A Bibliographical Account of English Theatrical Literature from the Earliest Times to the Present Day.* London: John C. Nimmo, 1888.
This bibliography list books, articles, periodicals, and newspapers on the theater. Plays and drama criticism are not included. Arrangement is alphabetical by author. Entries include annotations. A list of theatrical pseudonyms and initials is included. Updated by Arnott and Robinson's *English Theatrical Literature, 1559-1900: A Bibliography* (item 582).

585. *The Player's Library: The Catalogue of the Library of the British Drama League.* London: Faber and Faber, 1950.

The main feature of this catalog for the researcher in Victorian drama is its list of plays, many Victorian or adapted from Victorian writings. Unfortunately, dates are not included. The catalog includes an author section, a subject section, a title index, and an index of names.

586. Loewenberg, A. *The Theatre of the British Isles, Excluding London: A Bibliography.* London: Printed for the Society for Theatre Research, 1950.

This bibliography lists books describing theaters and theatrical performances of all kinds in all parts of the British Isles outside London, and in all periods. The first, general section is arranged chronologically; the second section is arranged by place and then chronologically. Author index.

587. British Museum. Catalogue of Additions to the Manuscripts. *Plays Submitted to the Lord Chamberlain 1824-1851: Additional Manuscripts 42865-43038.* London: The Trustees of the British Museum, 1964.

Though the contents of this volume are included in the *Index of Manuscripts in the British Library* (item 32), the usefulness of a separate volume devoted to the plays submitted to the Lord Chamberlain for licensing means that it is still an important aid to manuscript research on drama. Arrangement is chronological, with author and title indexes. References are to the bound volumes of plays now in the British Library.

588. Stratman, Carl J., comp. *Bibliography of English Printed Tragedy, 1565-1900.* Carbondale and Edwardsville, Southern Illinois University Press; London and Amsterdam: Feffer and Simons, 1966.

This bibliography gives the names, authors, imprints, pagination, library symbols, and some notes for 1483 English-language plays published in England between 1565 and 1900. Shakespeare's plays are not included, but a large amount of nineteenth century material is. Arrangement is alphabetical by author, with an added list of anthologies and collections listed by editor or title. Also included are a chronological list of the tragedies listed, a title index, and a listing, by author, of manuscripts of English printed tragedies.

589. Coleman, Arthur, and Gary R. Tyler. *Drama Criticism; A Checklist of Interpretation Since 1940 of English and American Plays.* 2 vols. Denver: Alan Swallow, 1966.

This set is a checklist of criticism on English-language drama of all periods. The criticism appeared between 1940-1964. The list includes both books and periodical articles.

590. Stratman, Carl J. "Dramatic Play Lists, 1591-1963." *Bulletin of the New York Public Library* (Feb.-March 1966): 169-88.

This article is a critical listing of bibliographies of play titles. Useful within its date limitations.

591. Hunter, Frederick J., comp. *Drama Bibliography: A Short-Title Guide to Extended Reading in Dramatic Art for the English-Speaking Audience and Students in Theatre.* Boston: G.K. Hall, 1971.
This bibliography covers material on theater up to September 1970. Arrangement is topical (Reference Works; Periodicals; Dramatic Literature; Selected Sources in Theatre History; Biography and Autobiography), with subdivisions by nationality and period. Index of persons.

592. Stratman, Carl J. *Britain's Theatrical Periodicals, 1720-1967: A Bibliography.* New York: The New York Public Library, 1972.
This chronological list of British theatrical periodicals covers over 1,000 periodicals appearing between 1720 and 1967. The introduction gives a brief history of dramatic periodicals in Britain. The list includes title, place of publication, dates, frequency, and libraries holding the title. A list of references and an index by title complete the book.

593. DuBois, William R., comp. *English and American Stage Productions: An Annotated Checklist of Prompt Books, 1800-1900, From the Nisbet-Snyder Drama Collection, Northern Illinois University Libraries.* Boston: G.K. Hall, 1973.
This checklist covers an important collection of plays from all periods, with annotations from nineteenth-century directors and actors. Organization is alphabetical by author of play, with about 100 plays of unknown authorship listed by title. Entries include: full title, number of pages in text, size in centimeters, series statement, physical appearance, summary of notations, and earliest recorded production. Indexes to authors, to titles, and to names.

594. Wells, Stanley, ed. *English Drama (Excluding Shakespeare); Select Bibliographic Guides.* Oxford: Oxford University Press, 1975.
This volume of bibliographic essays includes Michael R. Booth's chapter "Nineteenth-Century Drama." Recommended anthologies and general criticism are listed, as well as work on individual dramatists.

595. Thompson, Lawrence S. *Nineteenth- and Twentieth-Century Drama: A Selective Bibliography of English Language Works.* Boston: G.K. Hall. 1975.
This bibliography is the first part of an intended comprehensive listing of English-language drama of the nineteenth century. However, no further volumes have appeared, so the existing volume is scant and uneven in coverage. All types of dramatic literature are included. Entries give citations plus the number of pages. Indexing by title, subject, editors, joint authors, translators, pseudonyms, illustrators, and composers. It also gives information on finding microfiche copies of the works.

596. Conolly, Leonard W., and J. Peter Wearing, eds. *English Drama and Theatre, 1800-1900.* Detroit: Gale, 1978.
This bibliography covers nineteenth century English drama and theater. The first two chapters cover general criticism, chapter 1 from contemporary sources and chapter 2 from modern sources. Chapter 3 covers, in alphabetical order, major dramatists of the period. Other chapters cover bibliographies and reference works, anthologies of plays, the theaters, acting and management, the critics, stage design, scenic art and costume, and periodicals. The general index covers personal and geographic names as well as general subject areas and titles but could use more cross-references to connect persons, anonymous titles, and subjects. Coverage through 1973. Good starting place, but selective in its coverage.

597. Wearing, Peter J., ed. *American and British Theatrical Biography.* Metuchen, N.J.: Scarecrow, 1979.
This directory lists sources of biographical information for English and American persons connected with the theater. This connection is liberally interpreted, so that those who wrote plays but are better known for other writings (Dickens, Tennyson) are included. Each entry includes name, with cross-references to stage names and pseudonyms; dates of birth and death, nationality, theatrical occupation, and a code to the sources containing fuller information.

598. Johnson, Claudia D., and Vernon E. Johnson, comps. *Nineteenth-Century Theatrical Memoirs.* Westport, Conn.: Greenwood Press, 1982.
This bibliography lists memoirs, journals, and autobiographies of people involved in show business in Great Britain and the United States. Works are listed alphabetically under the stage name of the author. Annotations give an idea of contents and subsequent editions are noted. Author and subject index.

599. Field, James J. *The Book of World-Famous Libretti: The Musical Theater From 1598 to Today.* New York: Pendragon Press, 1984.
This book lists alphabetically information about the original libretti of 168 operas and musicals. The Gilbert and Sullivan operettas are included, as is Balfe's *The Bohemian Girl.* In addition to a description of the original libretto and the circumstances of its publication, a reproduction of the original title page is included. Supplements serve as indexes and offer further useful information: Librettist List; Composer List; Chronological List. Invaluable for performance studies.

Indexes

600. Firkins, Ina Ten Eyck, comp. *Index to Plays, 1800-1926.* New York: Wilson, 1927.
This index lists separately published plays, plays from collections, and plays in periodicals. The first part of the index is by author, the second by title and subject.

601. *Play Index.* New York: Wilson, 1953- . Irregular supplements.
This index began in 1953 and covered collections of plays published between 1949-1952. Supplements appeared at irregular intervals. Part I lists plays by author, title, and subject. The author entry is the main entry, giving the collection in which the play appears, publisher, date, and paging. A short description gives the number of acts and scenes, size of cast, number of sets required, copyright date, and brief plot summary. Part II lists collections indexed. Part III is a cast analysis index, and Part IV a directory of publishers.

602. Samples, Gordon. *Drama Scholars' Index to Plays and Filmscripts: A Guide to Plays and Filmscripts in Selected Anthologies, Series, and Periodicals.* Metuchen, N.J.: Scarecrow, 1974.
These two volumes index a wide range of English and foreign language books and periodicals covering plays and play criticism. Several Victorian authors are covered and many twentieth century dramatic adaptions of Victorian novels and short stories. Arrangement is by title and author in one alphabet, with complete information under author only.

603.   Connor, Billie M., and Helene G. Mochedlover.
         *Ottemiller's Index to Plays in Collections: An
         Author and Title Index to Plays Appearing in
         Collections Published Between 1900 and 1985.*
7th ed. revised and enlarged. Metuchen, N.J.:
Scarecrow, 1988.
This index lists the contents of collections of plays
published in the United States and England between 1900
and 1985. The main section is alphabetical by author and
includes the author's name and dates, title of the play, date
of first production, and a list of books containing this play.
Other sections are a List of Collections Analyzed, a key to
Symbols, and a Title Index.

Production   Lists

604.   Wearing, J.P. *London   Stage,   1890-1899: A
         Calendar of Plays and Players.* Metuchen, N.J.:
         Scarecrow, 1976.
This set is a daily listing of professional plays and players
appearing in London from 1890 to 1899. The information
is drawn from playbills arranged by date of opening
performance. Entries include title of play, genre, number
of acts and scenes, authors, theater or theaters in which
play was performed, date, length of run and number of
performances, cast (with substitutes and replacements
when known), production staff, short bibliography of first
night reviews, and comments. Thoroughly indexed.

605.   Mullin, Donald, comp. *Victorian Plays: A Record of
         Significant Productions on the London Stage,
         1837-1901.* Bibliographies and Indexes in the
         Performing Arts. New York: Greenwood, 1987.
This bibliography and compendium of information covers
legitimate plays and players appearing on the London stage
from 1837 to 1901. Cast lists include principal players
for the first performance. Index of playwrights, adaptors,
and translators.

Lists of Names and Biographical Sources

General

606. *Who's Who: An Annual Biographical Dictionary. With Which is Incorporated Men and Women of the Time.* London: Black; New York: St. Martin's, 1849-   . Annual.

This biographical dictionary began in 1849 and is still one of the most important sources for information about prominent living persons, chiefly British. From 1849 to 1897, it listed the names of those in the titled and official classes but did not include biographical material. In 1897, it began listing biographical information on prominent persons of all ranks. Biographies of deceased persons from 1897 on are compiled selectively in *Who Was Who* (item 614).

607.   *Men of the Time: A Dictionary of Contemporaries Containing Biographical Notices of Eminent Characters of Both Sexes.* London: D. Bogue, 1852. Title and publisher vary. Editions 1-14, 1852-1895.

This biographical dictionary contains sketches on living men and women famous for intellectual, political, and artistic achievement. The entire set forms a list of prominent Victorians, including some foreigners well-known to the British during this period.

608. Cooper, Thompson. *Men of Mark: A Gallery of Contemporary Portraits.* 7 vols. London: Sampson Low, Marston, Searle, and Rivington, 1876-1883.

These volumes give biographical sketches accompanied by photographs by Lock and Whitfield. Most of the entries are on British notables, with a few famous Europeans.

609. Ward, Thomas Humphrey, ed. *Men of the Reign: A Biographical Dictionary of Eminent Persons of British and Colonial Birth Who have Died during the Reign of Queen Victoria.* Groz, Austria: Akademische Druck, 1968. Reprt 1885 ed.

The subtitle of this volume leaves little to explain. *Men of the Time* (see item 607), obituaries in *The Times, The Athenaeum,* and other journals, and various biographical dictionaries were used as sources. The 3000 entries include name, dates, and brief biographies.

610. *Eminent Persons: Biographies Reprinted from "The Times."* London: Macmillan, 1892. Supplements 1891-1892, 1893-1894.

These articles reprinted from *The Times* cover a wide range of prominent Victorians. Some are feature articles, some obituaries. A rich source.

611. Boase, Frederic. *Modern English Biography: Containing Many Thousand Concise Memoirs of Persons Who Have Died Between the Years 1815-1900, with an Index of the Most Interesting Matter.* 3 vols and 3 supplements. London: Frank Cass & Co., Ltd., 1965. Reprt 1892 ed.

The six volumes of this work contain over 30,000 short biographical sketches of people who died between 1851 and 1900. Entries include sources used and a listing of photographs and portraits of the subject.

612. Plarr, Victor G. *Men and Women of the Time: A Dictionary of Contemporaries.* 15th ed. London: George Routledge and Sons, 1899.

This book and its earlier editions give brief biographies of important people of all nationalities. The emphasis, however, is on British notables and on foreigners well known in Britain during this period.

613. Stephen, Leslie and Sidney Lee, eds. *The Dictionary of National Biography.* London: Oxford University Press, 1908-. Reprinted 1921-22, 1937-38, 1949-50, 1959-60, 1963-64. 1st supplement, 1901; 2nd supplement, 1901-11; 3rd supplement, 1912-21; 4th supplement, 1922-30; 5th supplement, 1931-40; 6th supplement, 1941-50; 7th supplement, 1951-60; 8th supplement, 1961-70, 1971-80.

Lee, Sidney, ed. *Index and Epitome.* 2 vols. London: Smith, Elder, 1903-13.

The single most important source for British biography needs no introduction to scholars. Articles are signed by the author. Each supplement includes a cumulative index covering all entries from 1901. Though the biographies are generally accurate, mistakes are bound to appear in a work of this size. Some of these mistakes have been corrected in the *Dictionary of National Biography Corrections and Additions, Cumulated from the "Bulletin of the Institute of Historical Research, University of London," Covering the Years 1923-1963.* (Boston: G.K. Hall, 1966). This volume cumulates corrections and additions which appeared in the *Bulletin* from Volume 1 (1923) to the end of Volume 36 (1963).

614. *Who Was Who: A Companion to Who's Who; Containing the Biographies of Those Who Died During the Period.* London: Black, 1929- . Dates covered: 1897-1915; 1916-1928; 1929-1940; 1941-1950; 1951-1960; 1961-1970; 1971-1980.

These volumes reprint the brief biographical sketches that originally appeared in *Who's Who.* Death dates are included and, in some instances, additional information bringing the last *Who's Who* entry up to date. Indexing for this set is provided in *Who Was Who: a Cumulated Index, 1897-1980* (London: Black; New York: St. Martin's, 1981).

Indexes to Biography

615. Riches, Phyllis M. *An Analytical Bibliography of Universal Collected Biography: Comprising Books Published in the English Tongue in Great Britain and Ireland, America, and the British Dominions.* London: The Library Association, 1934.

This work indexes biographical sources of every kind. The main part of the volume is alphabetical by name of subject. Other sections include a bibliography of books analyzed, a chronological index, a subject index, and a subject index of dictionaries.

616. *Biography Index: A Cumulative Index to Biographical Material in Books and Magazines.* New York: Wilson, 1946- . Quarterly, with annual cumulations; further cumulated every two years.

This serial indexes biographies appearing in monographs, collective biographies, and periodicals. It covers autobiographies, diaries, letters, memoirs, interviews, obituaries, fictionalized biographies, dramatized biographies, biographical poetry, and biographies. Arrangement is by the subject, with an index to professions and occupations. It is searchable online through Wilsonline and a CD-ROM is available for information beginning August 1984.

617. Hyamson, Albert M. *A Dictionary of Universal Biography of All Ages and of All Peoples.* 2nd ed. New York: Dutton, 1951.

This index covers 33 biographical sources, including the national biographies of most Western nations.

618. Hanham, H.J. "Some Neglected Sources of Biographical Information: County Biographical Dictionaries, 1890-1937." *Bulletin of the Institute of Historical Research* 34 (1961): 55-63.

This article describes and lists an often overlooked source of biographical information. Sources for major holdings of county biographical dictionaries are noted.

619. Simpson, Donald H. *Biography Catalogue of the Library of The Royal Commonwealth Society.* London: Royal Commonwealth Society, 1961. This catalog lists biographical books to the close of 1959 and biographical periodical articles to the autumn of 1960. The first section lists individual biographies alphabetically by subject. The second section lists "Collective Biography and Country Indexes," first listing general collective biographies by date, then collective biographies by country covered. Author index. The catalog is especially valuable for locating material on figures both famous and obscure who built and maintained the British Empire.

620. Ireland, Norma Olin. *Index to Women of the World from Ancient to Modern Times: Biographies and Portraits.* Westwood, Mass.: Faxon, 1970. This volume indexes 945 collective biographies of women of all times and places. Emphasis is on the Western world. Arrangement is alphabetical within subject categories (Women as Pioneers, Women in the Fine Arts). Indexed by name.

621. *Biography and Genealogy Master Index.* 2nd ed. 8 vols. Detroit: Gale, 1980. Supplements, 1981-

This index analyzes more than 350 biographical dictionaries. Arrangement is alphabetical by subject name. The names are listed in the form in which they appear in the indexed source, so one person may have more than one entry. The sources indexed generally give brief biographical sketches; many list further sources. Excellent for tracking down obscure figures, as well as the famous, from all fields. A microfiche version *Bio-Base* is available, and the index is searchable online through DIALOG files 287 and 288.

622.   Slocum, Robert B. *Biographical Dictionaries and Related Works.* 2nd ed. Detroit, Mich.: Gale, 1986.

This two volume set lists more than 16,000 sources. Entries are arranged in three main sections: Universal Biography, National or Area Biography, and Biography by Vocation. Each entry includes a citation and a brief description. Indexed by author, by title, and by subject.

Family and Genealogical Records

623.   *Debrett's Peerage and Baronetage.* London: Macmillan, 1713- . Annual. Title varies slightly. Publisher varies.

Some version of this directory has been published since 1713. It gives information on biography, arms, living children, living collateral branches, predecessors, and other information of genealogical interest on the peers, baronets, and knights of Great Britain.

624.   Burke, Sir John Bernard. *Burke's Genealogical and Heraldic History of the Peerage, Baronetage, and Knightage.* London: Burke, 1826- . Title, publisher, and frequency vary.

Generally called *Burke's Peerage,* this genealogic and heraldic history does not go back as far as *Debrett's.* It does, however, have the advantage of being the only currently published record of the peerage to give full lineage. Arrangement is alphabetical by title.

625.   *Burke's Irish Family Records.* London: Burke's Peerage Limited, 1899-. Titles and publishers differ.

This biographical and genealogical listing covers Irish families not in the heredity peerage or baronetage. From 1899 to 1958, the first four editions were entitled *Burke's Landed Gentry of Ireland.*

626. *Burke's Genealogical and Heraldic History of the Landed Gentry.* London: Burke's Peerage Limited, 1965-1969.
Though this genealogical guide started recently, it includes lineage information of use for research on earlier periods. Arrangement is by family name and seat.

Women's Studies

627. Banks, Olive. *The Biographical Dictionary of British Feminists.* Volume 1, 1800-1930. New York: New York University Press, 1985.
This biographical dictionary begins with an informative essay on the varieties of feminism. The entries are lengthy enough to do justice to complex subjects and include a brief but well-chosen bibliography of sources.

Politics and Government

628. Stenton, Michael. *Who's Who of British Members of Parliament: A Biographical Dictionary of the House of Commons.* Vol. 1, 1832-1885; Vol 2, 1886-1918. Atlantic Heights, N.J.: Humanities Press; Hassocks, England: Harvester, 1976.
This dictionary is based on *Dod's Parliamentary Companion.* In addition to the material from Dod, Stenton has added material on members' careers after their terms in Parliament. Entries are brief but complete recountings of political careers.

629. Malchow, Howard LeRoy. *Agitators and Promoters in the Age of Gladstone and Disraeli: A Biographical Dictionary of the Leaders of British Pressure Groups Founded Between 1865 and 1886.* New York: Garland, 1983.

This biographical dictionary covers about 3000 people involved in political pressure groups between 1865 and 1886. Groups are restricted to non-partisan, non-special interest groups, who did not seek to change "the basic constitutional structure of politics." The groups included were founded between the given dates and left published records of their memberships. The people included were the leaders of these groups. The book is in two sections. The first is an alphabetical listing of names with information on birth and death dates, occupation, residence, sources from which this information has been gathered, and group affiliation. The second section is an appendix by group with an alphabetical listing of names.

630. Baylen, Joseph, and Norbert J. Gossman, eds. *Biographical Dictionary of Modern British Radicals.* Vol. 2, 1830-1870. Sussex, England: Harvester, 1984.

This book contains almost 200 biographies of British Radicals. The articles were written by about eighty contributors and are signed. Indexed by name and by topic.

Ireland

631. Crone, John S. *A Concise Dictionary of Irish Biography.* New York: Longmans Green, 1928.

This biographical dictionary covers people from the Middle Ages to the publication date. Entries are short, including profession or other short identifier, birth and death places and dates, major accomplishments, and major events in the life.

632. Boylan, Henry. *Dictionary of Irish Biography.*
Dublin: Gill and Macmillan, 1978.
This selective biographical dictionary gives short articles
on major figures of Irish history.

Scotland

633. Chambers, R. *A Biographical Dictionary of Eminent
Scotsmen.* 5 vols. Glasgow: Blackie and Son,
1855.
This set is an updated version of a four volume work
originally published in 1834. The emphasis, therefore, is
on figures from before Victoria's reign. The fifth
supplementary volume covers those who died between the
appearance of the supplement and the publication of the
main part of the set and so offers the largest number of
biographies of interest to Victorianists.

634. Anderson, William. *The Scottish Nation: or The
Surnames, Families, Literature, Honours, and
Biographical History of the People of Scotland.*
Edinburgh: A. Fullarton, 1863.
This biographical dictionary lists eminent Scots of all
periods. Biographies are lengthy and are especially good
for identifying lines of descent.

Wales

635. Morgan, J. Vyrnwy, ed. *Welsh Political and
Educational Leaders in the Victorian Era.*
London: James Nisbet & Co., 1908.
This work provides biographies of Welsh politicians and
educators of the Victorian period.

636. Lloyd, John Edward, and William Llewelyn Davids,
      eds. *The Dictionary of Welsh Biography Down to
      1940.* London: The Honourable Society of
      Cymmrodorion, 1959.
This dictionary was originally published in Welsh under
the title *Y Bywgraffiadur Cymreig hyd 1940.* This
translated and corrected English edition offers short
biographies, covering major life events. Short
bibliographies include manuscript locations.

Pseudonyms and Anonyms

637. Cushing, William. *Anonyms: A Dictionary of
      Revealed Authorship.* Cambridge, Mass.:
      William Cushing, 1890.
This listing of anonymous works and authors covers both
British and American authors of all periods. Arrangement
is by anonymous title followed by the name of the author.
Indexed by author.

638. Sharp, Harold S., comp. *Handbook of Pseudonyms
      and Personal Nicknames.* 2 vols. and 2
      supplements. Metuchen, N.J.: Scarecrow, 1972.
This set is a comprehensive list covering pseudonyms and
nicknames from all times and fields. Arrangement is in one
alphabet, with pseudonyms and real names interfiled. Real
names are listed in all capital letters and serve as main
entries, with dates, brief identification, and a list of all
pseudonyms used. Foreign language pseudonyms are
translated.

Portraits

639. Lane, William Coolidge, and Nina E. Brown. *A.L.A. Portrait Index: Index to Portraits Contained in Printed Books and Periodicals.* Washington, D.C.: GPO, 1906.

Over one thousand titles are indexed in this volume. The authors estimate that between thirty-five and forty-five thousand portraits are listed. This is a good source for finding portraits of both major and minor Victorians, though the scope of the volume far exceeds the Victorian period. Arrangement is alphabetical by person portrayed, followed by a list of portrait sources for that person. Citations are abbreviated when the title is listed in the front of the volume. Some titles are not included in this list; in this case, a fuller citation is given.

MICROFORM SOURCES

Microform collections, both microfilm and microfiche, are probably the most underused resource in American libraries. They are neglected for two reasons. First, the contents of these collections often are not listed in the catalogs of the institutions that own them. Few libraries have the resources to provide complete cataloging for these sets, many of which include thousands of separate titles; in most library catalogs, they are listed by the set title, but the individual pieces in the collections are not given separate listings. Scholars looking for a particular title in the library catalog can therefore easily remain unaware that it is available in this format. This situation is improving as more and more major sets are being analyzed in databases such as OCLC and RLIN. And since many libraries take their cataloging information from one of these sources, more and more libraries will be able to provide these analytics.

The second reason for the neglect of microforms is that many scholars find microforms unpleasant to use. Though using microforms can be fatiguing and offers few of the aesthetic pleasures of books or manuscripts, microforms allow libraries to provide materials that would otherwise be available only through extensive travel. This availability is especially important to graduate students *and junior faculty who may not be in a position to visit distant archives and libraries.*

The following list of microform sets gives some idea of the riches available in this format. It is extremely selective. At least a hundred sets of potential interest to the Victorian scholar are now available and new sets are being announced constantly. The following list discusses some of the sources for discovering what exists in microform. It also covers the single most important set for the study of the Victorian period, The Nineteenth Century. *The remaining sets listed here fall into 3 categories: 1) Reference tools or compendia of reference tools; 2) Sets based on special or archival collections in one library or archive; and 3) Sets based on one of the bibliographies covered in this guide.*

Lists of Microforms

640. *National Register of Microform Masters.* Washington, D.C.: Library of Congress, 1965-1982. Irregular.
This location list of materials that have been filmed and for which master negatives exist is arranged alphabetically. Before 1970, organization was by the Library of Congress call number. A six volume cumulation for 1965-1975 exists, then coverage is yearly. After 1982, this data is included in the *National Union Catalog* (item 15).

641. The Center for Research Libraries. *Handbook.* Chicago: Center for Research Libraries, 1969- .
The Center for Research Libraries is a non-profit corporation established and operated by research institutions. It purchases many large microform projects, as well as other material, too expensive or too infrequently used for any one library to buy. The *Handbook* is a guide to its various collections and to its policies.

642. *Newspapers in Microform.* 7th ed. 2 vols. Washington, D.C.: Library of Congress, 1973. Annual supplement.
This location list of negative and positive microforms of thousands of newspapers includes 9,453 from foreign countries including Great Britain. Arrangement is by state and city or by country of origin.

643. *Guide to Microforms in Print. Author, Title. Guide to Microforms in Print. Subject.* Westport, Conn.: Microform Review, 1978- . Annual.
These volumes list microforms, excluding dissertations, currently available. They replace *Guide to Microforms in Print* (1961-77), *Subject Guide to Microforms in Print* (1962/63-77), and *International Microforms in Print.*

Microform Sets

644. *The Nineteenth Century: A Microfiche Library of Historical Sources in English for the Study of the Period, 1801-1900.* Cambridge: Chadwyck-Healey, 1986-.
This project will film nineteenth-century English-language books of research value, especially those published after 1845 and in danger of loss through deterioration or not generally available in their original forms. The set will be produced over 30 years and consists of a general collection and several special collections. The General Collection covers British, Colonial, and international political studies, social studies, economics, transport and communication, commerce and industry, philosophy and aesthetics, beliefs and religion, education, law and society, entertainment and leisure, and the family. Specialized sets include linguistics and publishing, the book trade and diffusion of knowledge, art and architecture, women writers, children's literature, and music.

Biography

645. *British Biographical Archive.* München: Saur,
      1984- . 1200 microfiche.
This collection cumulates in one alphabet 310 of the most
important English-language biographical reference works
published between 1601 and 1929. Victorian sources
include Adams' *Dictionary of English Literature* (1879),
Adams' *Celebrated Englishwomen of the Victorian Era*
(1884), Adams' *Celebrated Women Travelers of the 19th
Century* (1883), Allibone's *A Critical Dictionary of
English Literature and British and American Authors*
(1859-71), Anderson's *The Scottish Nation* (1862), *The
Dictionary of Architecture* (1892), and many more. The
first sixteen fiche list the source works and give their title
pages and introductory material. A rich source of Victorian
bibliography.

Business and Economics

646. *Goldsmiths'-Kress Library of Economic Literature.*
      New Haven, Conn: Research Publications,
      1974- . Segment 2: Printed Books, 1801-
      1850. Segment 3: Serials and Periodicals.
This collection reproduces books and serials held at the
Goldsmiths' Library of the University of London and titles
from the Kress Library of Harvard University not held by
Goldsmiths'. The collection includes a wide range of
subjects, such as European colonial expansion, corn laws,
and socialism. Access is through the guides to the set,
*Goldsmiths'-Kress Library of Economic Literature: A
Consolidated Guide to Segment II of the Microfilm
Collection.* A temporary guide for Segment 3 is being issued
as this unit is produced. The majority of these materials
are in English and were published in Britain or America.

Drama and Theater

647. *Nineteenth and Twentieth Century English and American Drama.* Cambridge, Mass.: General Microfilm Co., for Lexington, Ky.: Falls City Microform Co., 1964-75. 11,495 microfiche.
The first section of this series was produced on microcards from 1964 to 1971. This portion is based on Lawrence S. Thompson's *Nineteenth- and Twentieth- Century Drama: A Selective Bibliography of English Language Works; numbers 1-3029* (item 595), which serves as a guide to this portion of the set. From 1972, the set appeared on microfiche and covered a wider range of plays, including plays in English regardless of country, period, or original language. No guide exists for this section of the set, but both cards and fiche have eye-legible bibliographic information on their header strips.

648. *English and American Plays of the 19th Century.* New York: Readex, 1965- . Microprint and microfiche.
This project aims to film every available English and American play published during the nineteenth century, including often neglected dramatic forms, such as unperformed poetic plays, pantomime, and burletta. With about 13,000 plays completed, of which over 8,000 are British, finished collection will include over 28,000 plays. The British list of plays is based on but not confined to Allardyce Nicoll's Handlist of Plays in volumes 4 and 5 of *A History of English Drama* (item 581). Access to the collection is provided by the guide *English Drama of the Nineteenth Century: An Index and Finding Guide,* compiled by Joseph Donohue and James Ellis (New York: Readex Books, 1985). This guide has listings by title, author, variant title, translator, and, for musical works, composer. Useful appendices include women authors, privately printed plays, acting editions, and pseudonyms and their real-name equivalents.

649. *The Popular Stage: Drama in Nineteenth Century
England: The Frank Pettingell Collection of
Plays in the Library of the University of Kent
at Canterbury.* Brighton: Harvester, 1985- .
This microfilm set includes manuscripts, typescripts, and
printed materials from the collection of the English actor
Frank Pettingell (1891-1966). The largest part of the
collection was produced at the Britannia Theatre from
1845 to 1885. Access is through guides to individual
parts. A full listing will be produced with the last part.

Government Documents and Records

650. *British Government Publications Containing
Statistics, 1801-1965, on Microfilm.*
Cambridge: Chadwyck-Healey, 1973. 332
reels.
This microfilm project gives essential statistical
information drawn from British government publications.
It is a convenient and well-organized compendium of
otherwise scattered information. Titles are arranged
chronologically, one to a reel. An effort has been made not
to split years between reels. The leaders and trailers of
each reel give full bibliographical information on the
contents of that reel, including Command Numbers.
Information on title changes is also included.

651. Great Britain. Cabinet. *Photographic Copies of
Cabinet Letters in the Royal Archives, 1868-
1916.* London: Public Records Office, 1975. 13
reels.
This series started with reports by Prime Ministers to the
crown and was expanded to include other letters. The
material is in chronological order. The letters are
photographed as is, with no interpreting or supporting
material.

652. British Foreign Office. *Japan: Correspondence 1856-1905: Indexes and Guides.* Wilmington, Del.: Scholarly Resources, 1975.
This microfilm edition covers British Foreign Office records classes F.O. 46, F.O. 802, and F.O. 566. The printed index and guide lists material by personal name and subject and contains a chronological register.

653. *Changes of Government, Cabinet Reconstructions and Political Crisis, 1837-1901.* Brighton, Sussex: Harvester, 1980. 13 reels.
This microfilm set is drawn from a collection of files in the Royal Archives. It includes "correspondence between the Queen and her ministers and extracts from the Queen's journal and other relevant letters" (Publisher's note).
It is based on a collection begun by Prince Albert and continued by the Queen. The editors have supplemented this collection with other relevant material from the Archives. The first reel contains a list of the subjects covered on each reel. Each reel lists, by year, the documents included for each incident covered. Overall arrangement is chronological.

654. *British Statistical Blue Books.* Leiden, Netherlands: IDC. Microfiche.
Blue Books were published for the following colonies and years: Cape of Good Hope, 1821-1885; Ceylon, 1862-1938; Cyprus, 1880-1946; Gibraltar, 1828-1947; Grenada, 1860-1938; Hong Kong, 1844-1938; Ionian Islands, 1821-1863; Malta, 1823-1938; New South Wales, 1822-1894; New Zealand, 1840-1898; Straits Settlements, 1868-1938; Tasmania, 1822-1847; Turks Islands, 1852-1944. Some years are lacking from these runs in the fiche.

History

655. *London Directories From the Guildhall Library,*
     1677-1900. Woodbridge, Ct.: Research
     Publications, 1973. Group II, 1800-1855.
     Group III, 1855-1900. 22 reels.
This project reproduces London commercial directories
found in the Guildhall Library. An invaluable historical
resource, it lists businesses and residents of London.
Various directories are organized in different ways. The
arrangement of material on reels is chronological. The
collection up to 1855 is based on Charles W. Goss's
directory of the same name (see item 239).

656. *The People's History: Working Class Autobiographies.*
     Brighton, England: Harvester, 1986. Part I:
     1792-1889. Part II: 1890-1920.
This set is based upon *The Autobiography of the Working
Class: An Annotated Critical Bibliography* (item 172).
Arrangement is chronological, by earliest known edition
date. Reel I has a reel guide and author list for Part I; Reel
19 has a listing for Part II.

Language and Literature

657. *Victorian Fiction and Other Nineteenth Century
     Fiction.* N.p.: General Microfilm, 1967.
     Microfilm.
This set is based on but not limited to Sadleir's *XIX Century
Fiction* (see item 347). Sadleir's book provides the only
guide to this collection outside of a short-title list supplied
with each shipment.

658. *British Culture: Series One and Two.* Louisville,
Ky.: Lost Cause Press, 1956; 1972- . Series
one: 5,000 microfiche.

The first series includes 848 volumes on all aspects of
British eighteenth and nineteenth century culture; the
second series is selected from volume 3 of the *New
Cambridge Bibliography of English Literature* (see item
301). Fiche in both series are arranged alphabetically by
main entry. Both primary texts and critical works are
included.

659. *The Archives of British Publishers on Microfilm.*
Cambridge: Chadwyck-Healey, 1974- .
Microfilm.

This set includes the archives of important British
publishing houses. Each publisher is treated as a separate
unit. Each unit has its own guide, which introduces and
indexes the microfilm. All of the units are of interest to
Victorianists: George Routledge & Co., 1853-1901; Grant
Richards, 1897-1948; Harper & Brothers, 1817-1914;
House of Longmans, 1794-1914; Richard Bentley & Sons,
1829-1898; Kegan Paul, Trench, Trubner, & Henry S.
King, 1853-1912; Macmillan and Co., 1854-1924;
Swann Sonnenschein and Co., 1878-1911.

660. *English Gift Books and Literary Annuals, 1823-
1857.* Bishop's Stortford: Chadwyck-Healey:
Teaneck, N.J.: Somerset House, 1976- .

This project involves the filming of complete runs of
representative early Victorian gift books. Access to
individual works within the annuals is provided by Andrew
Boyle's *Index to the Annuals, 1820-1850* (item 294).
Titles are on the fiche alphabetically, then chronologically.
Header strips contain eye-legible bibliographical
information.

Periodicals

661. *Scientific and Technical Periodicals.* Woodbridge,
     Ct.: Research Publications, 1989- .
This film collection will include about 2,500 scientific and
engineering periodical titles indexed in the Royal Society of
London's *Catalogue of Scientific Papers, 1800-1900*
(item 532). Contents will include the proceedings and
transactions of various societies, as well as journals.

Religion

662. *Westminster Cathedral (London), Archives.* N.p.:
     MicroMethods, n.d. 54 reels.
This microfilm set contains the archives for the Catholic
Church in Great Britain and its agencies from the late
sixteenth century to the middle of the nineteenth century.
Indexing is included on the film. Of special interest to
Victorian scholars are the two reels containing registers of
birth, marriages, and deaths in the Archbishop of
Westminster's archive, 1729-1909.

663. The Pilgrim Trust. *Survey of Ecclesiastical
     Archives.* London: Pilgrim Trust, 1952.
This survey was started in 1946 as part of a report on the
archives of the Church of England. The survey is Part II of
this report. It lists, by diocese, the collections of archives.
Part I describes the methodology of the project, its scope,
arrangement, and the accessibility of the collections.

664. *The Literature of Theology and Church History.*
Lexington, Ky.: Lost Cause Press, 1976.
This microfiche set draws on the *New Cambridge Bibliography of English Literature* (item 301) for the works of English theologians, religious thinkers, and church leaders. The first group of fiche focuses on works from the nineteenth century.

Visual Arts

665. *The Royal Commonwealth Society Photographic Collection.* Leiden: The Netherlands: IDC, n.d. Microfiche.
This collection contains 44,000 pictures, taken from 1850 to the mid-1980s, relating to imperial and Commonwealth history. A printed guide arranged in geographical order accompanies the set. Record cards at the beginning of each collection, extensive catalog information with each photograph, and a portrait index on fiche are further finding aids.

666. *British Posters to 1988 in the Victoria and Albert Museum National Poster Collection.* Boston: G.K. Hall, 1989. 48 fiche.
This set traces the history of the poster in Britain from trade cards and placards appearing in 1823 to modern posters. Arrangement is by artist, then by date of publication. A catalog, also arranged by artist, gives information on the artist, subject, medium, size, and description. Subject index.

Women's Studies

667. The Gertrude Tuckwell Collection, 1890-1920,
    From Congress House, London. Woodbridge,
    Conn.: Research Publications, n.d. 17 reels.
This collection covers the rise of the labor and women's
movements in Britain. The Gertrude Tuckwell Collection,
housed in the Trades Union Congress Library, consists of
Tuckwell's collection of press cuttings and pamphlets on
these movements, gathered between 1890-1920. Access is
through a thematic listing of files on the first reel. More
than 700 topics are assigned.

668. Voices of the Women's Movement: The Helen
    Blackburn Collection. Woodbridge, Conn.:
    Research Publication, n.d. 29 reels.
This two part collection is based on Helen Blackburn's
personal archive of pamphlets and other materials on the
women's movement in Britain and other nations in the late
nineteenth century. Most of the material here is
unavailable in other formats. Especially valuable and hard
to obtain are the conference reports from suffrage
societies. Access is through a guide indexed by author,
title, and subject. Part I is called "Pamphlets on Women's
Suffrage, The International Women's Movement and Related
Issues;" Part II covers "Pamphlets on the Employment of
Women,Women's Industries and Related Issues."

669. *The Cornell University Collection of Women's Rights Pamphlets.* Wooster, Ohio: Bell & Howell, 1974. 124 microfiche.
This collection reproduces 117 pamphlets published between 1814 and 1912. Most are British and American, with a few French pamphlets. Though the material is unique and valuable, the collection is a problem for the researcher because of its lack of indexing. Access is through the *Contents Guide to Cornell University Collection of Women's Rights Pamphlets* (Wooster, Ohio: Bell & Howell, 1974), in which the contents of the collection are listed in chronological order with an abstract of the contents, in alphabetical order by author, and alphabetically by organization. No subject access is provided.

670. *The Gerritsen Collection of Women's History (1543-1945).* Glen Rock, N.J.: Microfilming Corporation of America, 1976- . Approximately 16,000 microfiche.
This collection reproduces over 4,000 books, pamphlets, periodicals, and serials in The Kenneth Spencer Research Library collection at the University of Kansas. The focus of the collection is British and American women between 1850 and 1920, but the collection includes material from other periods and European nations. The material is divided into fourteen categories and then listed chronologically. The guide, *The Gerritsen Collection of Women's History: A Bibliographic Guide to the Microfilm Collection* (Glen Rock, N.J.: Microfilming Corporation of American, 1977) is a model of its kind, including access by main entry, author, title, subject, chronology, and country of imprint.

671. *History of Women, 1795-1920.* Woodbridge: Conn.: Research Publications, 1976-1983. 1,248 reels.

This collection is divided into five parts: printed books (reels 1-934), pamphlets (reels 935-962), periodicals (reels P1-P253), manuscripts (reels 964-995), and photographs (reel 963). The collection is based on the Arthur and Elizabeth Schlesinger Library on the History of Women in America and the Sophia Smith Collection. Emphasis is on the history of American women, but a substantial amount of the material comes from Victorian Britain. Access is through the printed guide, *History of Women: Guide to the Microfilm Collection* (Woodbridge, Conn.: Research Publications, 1983). This guide gives reel guide summaries, a main entry index, a periodicals title list, a subject/added entry list, and a name index to photographs.

ELECTRONIC FORMATS

Guides and Lists

672. *Computer-Readable Databases: A Directory and Data Sourcebook.* Washington, D.C.: American Society for Information Science, 1979-. Publisher varies.

This database and its print equivalent list databases available worldwide. Each entry gives the database name and acronym, producer name, address, first date of availability, time covered, file size, update frequency, subject coverage, and other information on characteristics and availability. It can be searched for the current year as DIALOG file 230.

673. *Directory for Online Databases.* New York: Cuadra/Elsevier, 1980- . 2 directories and 2 updates a year.

This directory lists databases in two categories: reference databases, subdivided into bibliographic and referral databases, and source databases, subdivided into numeric and textual-numeric databases. Full-text databases and software programs are also listed. Entries give the subject covered by the database, the producer, vendors, a lengthy note on context, language, nations covered, time span, and frequency of updates. Some entries also list special conditions for subscription. Subject, producer, online service/gateway, telecommunication, and master indexes.

674.   *CD-ROMs in Print.* Eastport, Conn.: Meckler Corp.,
       1987- . Annual.
This annual lists currently produced CD-ROMs, their cost,
the company producing them, and the hard- and software
necessary for running them.

Major Vendors of Online Databases

675. BRS. McLean, Virginia: BRS Information
      Technologies. Account information: 800-468-
      0908.
BRS offers several online services providing access to
bibliographic, numeric, and full-text databases. BRS
Search Service is available 22 hours a day Monday through
Saturday and nineteen hours on Sunday. It offers over 150
databases and is searchable both in command language and
through menus. BRS After Dark is a reduced-rate service
available on evenings and weekends. It is limited to fewer
databases than the full search service and is entirely
menu-driven. Though the emphasis of these services is on
medical databases, it also offers a selection from education,
science, social science, humanities, business, and
reference. Information on the databases offered is listed in
this guide under the individual index name.

676.   DIALOG. Palo Alto, Ca.: DIALOG Information Service.
       Account information: 800-3-DIALOG.
DIALOG offers over 300 databases. It is available 24 hours
a day, six days a week. On Sunday, it is available for eleven
hours. The full DIALOG service is command driven and
requires extensive training and experience for its most
effective use. Its after-hours service, Knowledge Index,
uses either command language or menu. It includes about
60 of DIALOG's databases.

677. Wilsonline. New York: H. W. Wilson. Account information: 800-367-6770.
Wilsonline provides online access to 21 indexes produced by the H.W. Wilson Company and four other indexes originating with other companies. All databases can be searched by subject, author, and title, plus additional access points varying with the database. Boolean operators can be used. Access is generally available 24 hours a day, seven days a week. Wilson also offers a number of CD-ROMs based on some of these databases.

Bibliographic Utilities

678. RLIN (Research Libraries Information Network)
OCLC (Online Computer Library Center)
These two bibliographic databases are the most commonly used facilities for acquisitions, cataloging, and interlibrary loan information in American academic libraries. Some libraries provide public access terminals, and scholars can subscribe individually to them. The two networks carry much overlapping information, though there are some differences in the libraries they cover. Both include Library of Congress records, National Library of Canada records, and British Library records. The search methods for these two systems are entirely different and best learned once you find you will be using that particular database.

In addition to its library records, RLIN has two other parts: Library of Congress name and subject authority files and these special databases: *Avery Index to Architectural Periodicals, Avery Reference, ESTC-Eighteenth Century Short-Title Catalogue,* R I P D— Research-in-Progress Data Base, RLG Conspectus On-line, SCIPIO—Sales Catalog Index Project Input On-line.

INDEX

(Numbers in index indicate entry numbers)